Translating for the European Union Institutions

Emma Wagner
Svend Bech
Jesús M. Martínez

St. Jerome Publishing
Manchester, UK & Northampton, MA

Published by
St. Jerome Publishing
2 Maple Road West, Brooklands
Manchester, M23 9HH, United Kingdom
Tel +44 161 973 9856
Fax +44 161 905 3498
stjerome@compuserve.com
http://www.stjerome.co.uk

ISBN 1-900650-48-7 (pbk)
ISSN 1470-966X (*Translation Practices Explained*)

Printed and bound in Great Britain by
T. J. International Ltd., Cornwall, UK

Cover design by
Steve Fieldhouse, Oldham, UK (+44 161 620 2263)

Cover logo created by Alain Senez (www.alainsenez.com)

Typeset by
Delta Typesetters, Cairo, Egypt
Email: delttyp@starnet.com.eg

British Library Cataloguing in Publication Data
A catalogue record of this book is available from the British Library

Library of Congress Cataloging-in-Publication Data
Wagner, Emma.
  Translating for the European Union institutions / Emma Wagner, Svend Bech, Jesús M. Martínez.
    p. cm. -- (Translation practices explained, ISSN 1470-966X)
Includes bibliographical references (p.) and index.
  ISBN 1-900650-48-7
  1. Translating and interpreting--Europe. 2. European Union. 3.
Multilingualism. I. Bech, Svend. II. Martínez, Jesús M. III. Title.
IV. Series.
  P306.8.E85 W34 2001
  418'.02'094--dc21
                              2001003939

Translation Practices Explained

Translation Practices Explained is a series of coursebooks designed to help self-learners and teachers of translation.

Each volume focuses on a specific type of translation, in most cases corresponding to actual courses available in translator-training institutions. Special volumes are devoted to professional areas where labour-market demands are growing: court interpreting, community interpreting, European-Union texts, multimedia translation, text revision, electronic tools, and software and website localization.

The authors are practising translators or translator trainers in the fields concerned. Although specialists, they explain their professional insights in a manner accessible to the wider learning public.

Designed to complement the *Translation Theories Explained* series, these books start from the recognition that professional translation practices require something more than elaborate abstraction or fixed methodologies. The coursebooks are located close to work on authentic texts, simulating but not replacing the teacher's hands-on role in class. Self-learners and teachers are encouraged to proceed inductively, solving problems as they arise from examples and case studies. The series thus offers a body of practical information that can orient and complement the learning process.

Each volume includes activities and exercises designed to help self-learners consolidate their knowledge and to encourage teachers to think creatively about their classes. Updated reading lists and website addresses will also help individual learners gain further insight into the realities of professional practice.

Anthony Pym
Series Editor

Contents

Introduction

> "After three days Demetrius took the men with him and crossed the break-
> water, seven stades long, to the island; then he crossed over the bridge
> and proceeded to the northerly parts. There he called a meeting in a man-
> sion built by the seashore, magnificently appointed and in a secluded
> situation, and called upon the men to carry out the business of transla-
> tion, all necessary appliances having been well provided. And so they
> proceeded to carry it out, making all details harmonise by mutual com-
> parisons. The appropriate result of the harmonisation was reduced to
> writing under the direction of Demetrius. The sessions would last until
> the ninth hour, and afterwards they would break up to take care of their
> bodily needs, all their requirements being lavishly supplied."
>
> 'Aristeias' (around 130 B.C.) (in Robinson 1997:5-6)

So an Ancient Greek writer describes how seventy-two translators were sum-
moned from the tribes of Israel and installed on the island of Pharos, near
Alexandria, to translate the biblical law of the Jews into Greek. The undertaking had been ordered by royal decree of King Ptolemy II. This ancient version
of events subsequently evolved into the legend of the Septuagint: the 70 schol-
ars who produced the sacred translations of the Old Testament.

The number of translators employed by the European Union institutions is
many more than seventy-two and we are not all men. Our places of work, Brussels and Luxembourg, may indeed be in "northerly parts" – depending on your
point of view – but unfortunately they are not by the seashore. Nor can our
offices be described as "mansions magnificently appointed". Yet we humbly
submit that we are continuing the business of translation in the tradition started
by the Seventy-Two, "using all necessary appliances and making all details
harmonise by mutual comparisons". Work may often continue until the ninth
hour and beyond, but no one could claim that our requirements are not lavishly
supplied.

* * *

This book is about translation for the European Union institutions and it is intended for all translators, in-house, freelance and aspiring, whose translation
work may touch on the activities of those institutions. Our subject is the written
translation of documents; we do not attempt to describe arrangements for oral
translation of speech – or **interpreting** as it is generally known, to distinguish it
from written **translation**. Much of what we say about the EU institutions and

their language requirements will be of interest to interpreters, however.

This book is itself a translation, in part, and is a typically European endeavour. It was written by three translators at the European Commission: Emma Wagner (an English translator), Svend Bech (a Danish translator) and Jesús M. Martínez (a Spanish translator). Because the three authors work at the European Commission, many of the examples and anecdotes relate to the situation there. Nevertheless, one of the purposes of the book is to emphasise that there are several different institutions, each with its own responsibilities and its own translation service; and accordingly, every effort has been made to provide information that is representative of all the institutions.

Sources and acknowledgments

So many sources have been used in compiling this book that it would be tedious to mention them at each occurrence. Those most often used and sometimes quoted with little or no amendment include the Europa server (http://europa.eu.int), the Interinstitutional Directory (*Who's who in the European Union?*) produced by the Office for Official Publications, articles by our Director-General Brian McCluskey and our former Director-General Colette Flesch, our former Adviser on Enlargement Archie Clarke, information brochures on the translation services, and the English Style Guide. Much of the material has been gleaned from our fellow translators over the years, and we particularly thank the following for allowing us to recycle their ideas and anecdotes: Renato Correia at the European Parliament, and Bill Fraser and Robert Rowe at the European Commission.

We are indebted to the following people for checking part or all of the contents: the Directors and Directors-General of translation in all the institutions; Jens Christoffersen in the Commission's Legal Service; Pascale Berteloot at the European Court of Justice; Rebecca West at the Translation Centre; Stephen Harrison at the Court of Auditors; Tim Martin, Roger Bennett, Raffaella Longoni, Vassili Koutsivitis and Bill Bythell in the Commission's Translation Service; and Andrew Chesterman at Helsinki University. We also thank Jane Gehrke and Morag Reinert for their prompt and cheerful secretarial assistance.

Lastly, we thank our editor, Anthony Pym, for his help and forbearance throughout the project. All remaining errors are our own. The views presented here are those of the authors and not necessarily those of the European Commission.

How to use this book

Some chapters can be used for reference: Chapter 1 explains the legal basis of translation and multilingualism, while Chapter 2 summarises the roles of the EU institutions and the correct (and incorrect) ways to refer to them. Other chapters give information on recruitment, work content, problems frequently encountered, work organisation, and the impact of EU enlargement on translation work.

The final chapter presents profiles of some translators and translation users; it places the information provided in the earlier chapters in a real-life context.

Most chapters are followed by a section entitled "Exercises for students", which is intended for students of translation who have English as their mother tongue or first foreign language. The exercises are designed to be fairly enjoyable, typical of the skills ideally required (with a strong emphasis on computer skills), and easy to assess. Proficiency in these exercises will not however guarantee a job with the EU institutions. The prime qualification is still that enigma: a talent for translation.

House style
By agreement with the publishers, this book does not adhere to the spelling and punctuation conventions normally followed in the St Jerome series. Instead we use the house style of the EU institutions as set out in the English Style Guide at http://europa.eu.int/comm/translation/en/stygd.

1. Why we translate

During its brief history, the European Union has grown greatly in terms of the area it covers, its political significance and its institutions. The founding Treaties of 1951 and 1957 have been revised several times: in 1987 (the Single European Act), in 1992 (the Treaty on European Union, signed at Maastricht) and in 1997 (Treaty of Amsterdam). In December 2000 some further changes were proposed in the Treaty of Nice.

The ultimate goal of the European Union is "an ever closer union among the peoples of Europe, in which decisions are taken as openly as possible and as closely as possible to the citizen" (Article 1 of the Treaty on European Union). It aims to promote economic and social progress that is balanced and sustainable, to assert the European identity on the international scene and to introduce a European citizenship for the nationals of the Member States.

One of the provisions of the Treaty on European Union, laid down in Article 6, is that

> *"The Union shall respect the national identities of its Member States"*.

The European Union institutions exist to serve the EU and its citizens, a community of peoples with a fascinating variety of customs, characteristics – and languages.

Multilingualism: the principle

In the context of the European Union, the word "multilingual" has taken on a meaning that goes beyond its dictionary definition of "speaking or using many languages", or "written or printed in many languages". For us, multilingualism is a fundamental principle with the additional meaning of "equal rights for all official languages".

Equal status for the official languages goes to the heart of what the European Union is all about. Language is a part of national and personal identity. There can be no question of imposing a sort of artificial "Euro-identity" – far from it: the languages of Europe are part of its immense and diverse cultural heritage, and they should be cherished.

At the outset in the 1950s there were six Member States: Belgium, France, Germany, Italy, Luxembourg and the Netherlands. Between them they had four official languages: Dutch, French, German and Italian.

Now, after the most recent accessions in 1995, the European Union has 15 Member States:

> Austria, Belgium, Denmark, Finland, France, Germany, Greece, Ireland, Italy, Luxembourg, the Netherlands, Portugal, Spain, Sweden and the United Kingdom.

and 11 official languages:

> Danish, Dutch, English, Finnish, French, German, Greek, Italian, Portuguese, Spanish and Swedish

It is fair to ask why we need so many official languages. Why can't we manage with a smaller number, like the United Nations, UNESCO, NATO, OECD and other international organisations?

The answer is to be found in the word "Union" (previously "Community"), which denotes a much deeper level of integration than the intergovernmental cooperation taking place in organisations like the UN. The ambition of the European Union is to be a "Union of Citizens". Its institutions produce legislation that is directly applicable to all citizens in all the Member States and must therefore be available in their official languages.

Equality before the law

The need for **certainty as to the law** is the first reason why translation plays such a large part in the activities of the European institutions.

Article 249 of the Treaty establishing the European Community (EC Treaty) describes the different types of legal instrument produced by the European Union institutions:

> "In order to carry out their task and in accordance with the provisions of this Treaty, the European Parliament acting jointly with the Council, the Council and the Commission shall make regulations and issue directives, take decisions, make recommendations or deliver opinions.
> A regulation shall have general application. It shall be binding in its entirety and directly applicable in all Member States.
> A directive shall be binding, as to the result to be achieved, upon each Member State to which it is addressed, but shall leave to the national authorities the choice of form and methods.
> A decision shall be binding in its entirety upon those to whom it is addressed.
> Recommendations and opinions shall have no binding force."

As Article 249 shows, the different types of instrument are binding in different ways. **Regulations** are binding in their entirety and directly applicable in all the

Member States; **Decisions** are binding on those to whom they are addressed; **Directives** are *binding, as to the result to be achieved*, upon each Member State to which they are addressed. The precise methods of achieving these results are left to the Member States (*shall leave to the national authorities the choice of form and methods*).

The important point is that most of these instruments are binding in some way, and that is why they have to be translated. It is simply a matter of democracy. It is a legal obligation and a democratic necessity to present Community legislation to European citizens in their own language in order to guarantee equality before the law. Ignorance of the law is no defence, so the law cannot be imposed in an incomprehensible foreign language. Scottish whisky distillers, Danish civil servants, German industrialists, British barristers, Finnish students, French wine growers, Italian car designers and the rest must always have access to the European legislation affecting them. And they must have access to it in their own language.

The means of public access to Community law – and the place where many of our translations are published – is the **Official Journal of the European Communities** (re-named the "Official Journal of the European *Union*" in the Nice Treaty of December 2000). The Official Journal is the only periodical published every working day in all the official languages of the European Union. It is produced by the Office for Official Publications (EUR-OP) in paper and CD-ROM editions (for subscriptions and charges see EUR-OP's website <http://eur-op.eu.int/index>). Legislation can also be accessed, against payment, in the two online databases CELEX and EUDOR. An additional online service, EUR-Lex, is available free of charge at http://europa.eu.int/eur-lex.

But the final versions of legislation published in the Official Journal are just the tip of the iceberg. Every legal act published is the outcome of a long process of discussion and negotiation. Proposals made by the Commission are normally based on cooperation with outside contacts – committees of national government experts, representatives of the private sector, universities and economic and social interests – whose opinions are required before any decision can be taken. Translation is needed at all the many stages in the preparation of Community legislation:

- preparing the working papers, which often include a substantial amount of technical documentation;
- examining the draft versions, which require extensive consultation;
- putting together the final text, which represents a commitment by the Commission and is likely to reach a broad spectrum of readers;
- preparing the written information that the Commission is required to circulate at all levels once its proposal has been adopted;
- discussing and amending the proposal in the European Parliament and Council prior to finalisation.

Citizenship of the Union

The European Union institutions are not there just to churn out regulations. Article 21 (third indent) of the EC Treaty states that:

> "Every citizen of the Union may write to any of the institutions or bodies referred to in this Article or in Article 7 in one of the languages mentioned in Article 314 and have an answer in the same language."
> (Article 7 lists the institutions; Article 314 names the official languages)

This provision was introduced by the Amsterdam Treaty, which was signed in 1997 and entered into force on 1 May 1999. It aims to give equal treatment to all European citizens regardless of their mother tongue. It means that every member of the European public is entitled to write to any of the institutions, for whatever reason, in the language of their choice – as long as it is one of the official languages – and to receive a reply in the same language.

Another new provision introduced by the Amsterdam Treaty, in Article 255 of the EC Treaty, was:

> "Any citizen of the Union [...] shall have a right of access to European Parliament, Council and Commission documents."

This also has obvious implications for translation; accessibility implies providing a version in a language the citizen can understand.

The number of official languages has grown gradually to the present number of 11 from the original four (Dutch, French, German and Italian, the languages of the original six Member States). In 1973 Denmark, Ireland and the United Kingdom joined, so Danish and English were added; in 1981 Greece joined, adding Greek; in 1986 Portugal and Spain brought Portuguese and Spanish, and in 1995, Austria, Finland and Sweden joined, bringing two more official languages: Finnish and Swedish.

When new Member States join, the Treaties are translated into the new official languages, and these new language versions are as "authentic" (legally valid) as the four initial versions. That is why the Treaties now exist in 11 language versions, or to be precise, in 12 languages, because there is also an Irish version. Irish is a Treaty language but not an official language or a working language of the institutions, although it may be used as an official language for cases in the European Court of Justice, and the Court's rules of procedure also exist in Irish.

People often ask why the official languages do not include all the languages spoken in the European Union. Why don't speakers of Welsh, Basque, Catalan and Breton have the same rights to use their languages for dealings with the institutions? This is a fair question, but the answer is that the "official language"

of each Member State is the one it has stipulated during the membership negotiations. The choice is not dictated by the EU institutions. The Member States
themselves have taken a political decision to keep the number of official languages within limits in order to minimise administrative difficulties and costs.
That is why the 15 Member States have only 11 official languages between
them: because several of them share one or more official languages with a neigh-
bouring country: Austria and Germany share German, Ireland and the United
Kingdom share English, and so on. (See also Article 8 of Council Regulation
No 1, quoted below.)

Legal basis of multilingualism

The Treaty of Paris, which set up the European Coal and Steel Community in
1951, did not mention multilingualism; this first Treaty was authentic only in
French. Nor did language matters and the policy of multilingualism feature in
the two Treaties of Rome signed in 1957, setting up the European Economic
Community and the European Atomic Energy Community (Euratom). All we
had in those Treaties was a brief provision to the effect that:

> "The rules governing the languages of the institutions of the Community
> shall (...) be determined by the Council, acting unanimously."
> (Article 217 of the EC Treaty, or Article 290 in the consolidated version.)

So, when the Treaties of Rome entered into force on 1 January 1958, the very
first Regulation adopted by the Council of national ministers (which was – and
still is – the supreme law-making body of the European Union) dealt with the
official languages and working languages to be used. The Regulation is given
below, in a simplified and "consolidated" version ("consolidated" = incorporat-
ing the successive amendments made since the Regulation was first adopted, in
this case reflecting the addition of new official languages until the most recent
enlargement of the European Union in 1995).

COUNCIL REGULATION No 1
determining the languages to be used by the European
Economic Community
(as amended)
THE COUNCIL OF THE EUROPEAN ECONOMIC COMMUNITY,

Having regard to Article 217 of the Treaty which provides that the rules
governing the languages of the institutions of the Community shall, without prejudice to the provisions contained in the rules of procedure of the
Court of Justice, be determined by the Council, acting unanimously;

Whereas each of the 11 languages in which the Treaty is drafted is recognised as an official language in one or more of the Member States of
the Community;

HAS ADOPTED THIS REGULATION:

Article 1
The official languages and the working languages of the institutions of
the Community shall be Danish, Dutch, English, Finnish, French, German, Greek, Italian, Portuguese, Spanish and Swedish.

Article 2
Documents which a Member State or a person subject to the jurisdiction
of a Member State sends to institutions of the Community may be drafted
in any one of the official languages selected by the sender. The reply
shall be drafted in the same language.

Article 3
Documents which an institution of the Community sends to a Member
State or to a person subject to the jurisdiction of a Member State shall be
drafted in the language of such State.

Article 4
Regulations and other documents of general application shall be drafted
in the 11 official languages.

Article 5
The Official Journal of the Community shall be published in the 11 official languages.

Article 6
The institutions of the Community may stipulate in their rules of procedure which of the languages are to be used in specific cases.

Article 7
The languages to be used in the proceedings of the Court of Justice shall
be laid down in its rules of procedure.

Article 8
If a Member State has more than one official language, the language to
be used shall, at the request of such State, be governed by the general
rules of its law.

This Regulation shall be binding in its entirety and directly applicable in
all Member States.
Done at Brussels, 15 April 1958.

> For the Council
> The President
>
> V. LAROCK

Council Regulation No 1 is in a sense our language charter. It lists the official languages (Article 1) and states that the Official Journal must be published in all these languages (Article 5). The right referred to in Article 2 – to write to the EU institutions in any official language, and to receive a reply in that language – has, as already explained, recently been enshrined in the Treaty as amended at Amsterdam in 1997.

Article 4 of Council Regulation No 1 refers to the feat of "drafting in 11 languages", an expression coined to avoid mentioning "translations". None of the legislation refers to translation. This is not a conspiracy to reduce translators' visibility; it is simply the logical consequence of the principle according to which all official languages have equal status.

The all-important concept of "equally authentic texts" in different languages is first encountered in the Final Provisions of the EC Treaty:

> "This Treaty, drawn up in a single original in the Dutch, French, German and Italian languages, **all four texts being equally authentic**, shall be deposited in the archives of the Government of the Italian Republic, which shall transmit a certified copy to each of the Governments of the other signatory States.
> Pursuant to the Accession Treaties, the Danish, English, Finnish, Greek, Irish, Portuguese, Spanish and Swedish versions of this Treaty shall also be **authentic.**
> In witness whereof, the undersigned Plenipotentiaries have signed this Treaty.
>
> Done at Rome this twenty-fifth day of March in the year one thousand nine hundred and fifty-seven."
>
> Article 314 of the Treaty establishing the European Community (EC Treaty), consolidated version (C 340 of 10 November 1997:302) [emphasis added]

The concept of multiple authenticity safeguards the equal rights of all languages and therefore the national identity of all Member States. It reflects the desire that there should be no dominant languages or cultures in the European Union.

It is at this point that translators may begin to feel some twinges of professional conscience. As good Europeans, we may subscribe to these laudable intentions, but as translators we know only too well that perfect equivalence of different language versions is impossible. This point is illustrated and discussed further in Chapter 5 – Problems. For the lawyers, however, multiple authenticity and "drafting in 11 languages" present no problems: if equal meaning is not possible, there should at least be equal effect; and if that does not arise, one can try to solve the problem by invoking equal intent. For the politicians, of course, equal respect for all official languages (i.e. countries) is a *sine qua non* of the European Union.

Language versions or translations?

Officially, then, for texts published in all the official languages, there are not "one original text and ten translations" but "11 language versions" or even "11 originals". Article 6 of Council Regulation No 1 refers to the rules of procedure of the Community institutions. It is interesting to quote some sections of the rules of procedure here, not least because they too avoid any reference to "translations" and refer instead to "language versions".

The European Parliament's rules of procedure do mention the existence of an original text, but only in order to stipulate that it is no more authoritative that the other language versions (and may even be less authoritative, if the President so decides):

European Parliament Rules of Procedure (14th edition – Official Journal L 202, 2 August 1999:1-108)
Rule 117 – Languages

> 1. All documents of Parliament shall be drawn up in the official languages.
> (...)
> Where it has been established after the result of a vote has been announced that there are discrepancies between different language versions, the President shall decide whether the result announced is valid (...). If he declares the result valid, he shall decide which version is to be regarded as having been adopted. However, the original version cannot be taken as the official text as a general rule, since a situation may arise in which all the other languages differ from the original text.

The European Commission's rules of procedure reflect the more differentiated approach at the Commission – unlike the European Parliament, the Commission does not require all documents to be available in all the official languages. It makes a distinction between instruments of general application (required in all languages) and other instruments that are for specific addressees and need only be available in the language or languages of those to whom they are addressed. In the following extract, and in the Final Provisions of the EC Treaty quoted above, the word "authentic" means "legally valid" rather than "original". The French version of "authentic language" is *langue faisant foi*.

Rules of Procedure of the Commission (Official Journal L 308, 8 December 2000:26)
Article 18

> Instruments adopted by the Commission in the course of a meeting shall be attached, in the authentic language or languages, in such a way that

they cannot be separated, to a summary note prepared at the end of the meeting at which they were adopted. They shall be authenticated by the signatures of the President and the Secretary-General on the last page of the summary note.

(...)

For the purposes of these Rules, "authentic language or languages" means the official languages of the Communities in the case of instruments of general application and the language or languages of those to whom they are addressed in other cases.

What's in a name? Whether they are producing "translations" or "language versions", translators play an important part in the workings of the European institutions and, together with interpreters, make up a large proportion of the institutions' staff. The next chapter explains what the different institutions do and gives some basic information about their translation services.

Before that, let's examine some myths about multilingualism.

Three common myths about multilingualism

Myth 1: All EU documents are translated into all the official languages.

This is not true. Certainly, all laws and many "outgoing" documents do have to be translated into all the official languages, because they are of general application and have to be published (Articles 4 and 5 of Council Regulation No 1, quoted above). But the situation is different for "incoming" documents of the type mentioned in Article 2 of Regulation No 1 – reports from Member States and correspondence from individuals, sent for processing within the institutions. It may be sufficient to translate these into one language for information (usually English or French), since all Eurocrats know English or French or else they learn them – fast. Common sense dictates that translations should only be produced if they are needed.

Myth 2: Multilingualism absorbs a huge proportion of the EU budget.

In 1999 the total cost of interpreting and translation services for all the institutions combined was €685.9 million (Reply to Parliamentary Question E-2239/99 by MEP Christopher Huhne). This is equivalent to €1.8 for each member of Europe's population of 374 million. About the same as a couple of newspapers.

Translation and interpreting form part of the administration budget, but administration absorbs only 5.25% of the total budget. The rest is spent on agriculture, external aid, jointly-funded research projects, etc. The cost of translation and interpreting in 1999, i.e. the figure of €685.9 million quoted above, was less than one sixth (15%) of the total administration budget and less than 1% of the total budget.

(Sources: Written Question E-2239/99: Official Journal C 219 E, 1 August 2000:219; calculations based on figures given in "The Community Budget: The facts in figures 2000", both available online on the Europa server.)

Myth 3: It would be easy to reduce the number of working languages.
The political significance of multilingualism and the difficulty of altering the language regime should not be underestimated. It is always possible to introduce unofficial restrictions in exceptional circumstances: it is rumoured that the Members of the Commission are capable of communicating in English when the topic is so confidential that the interpreters have to be sent out of the meeting room. Likewise, all Eurocrats are required to work in English and/or French, regardless of their mother tongue. Unnecessary translation and interpreting can often be avoided by informal arrangements. However, all proposals for *formal* reductions in the number of languages have been rejected by the Member States, because of national sensitivities and also for the legal reasons outlined above.

The same is true of attempts to introduce a distinction between "**official languages**" (for legislation, etc.) and "**working languages**" (for use in meetings). At present there is no official distinction between the two (see Article 1 of Council Regulation No 1 quoted above). In the European Commission, we do use the expression "**procedural languages**" to refer to English, French and German, because those are the languages in which documents have to be provided before they can be adopted at a meeting of the Commission. The eight "non-procedural" language versions must still be produced, but for a later deadline, usually 48 hours after the meeting. However, the concept of "procedural languages" has no basis in legislation or the rules of procedure.

When representatives of the Member States are discussing EU legislative proposals, they expect to have all the language versions, and political incidents may occur if they are not available. This point is mentioned by several translation users in the interviews at the end of this book.

Exercises for students

1. Why we translate

1.1   Research
1.1.1 Visit the Europa website (http://europa.eu.int) and find out where the Treaties are presented there.
1.1.2 Use CELEX, Eur-Lex or the paper version of the Official Journal to find Council Regulation No 1 in your working languages.

1.2   Terminology
1.2.1 Make a list of the names of the 15 Member States in all 11 official languages (use Europa to find the names).

1.2.2 The passage from Article 249 of the EC Treaty quoted in Chapter 1 mentions five types of legislative instrument that may be issued by the Council, Parliament and Commission. What are the five? Produce a three-language list or glossary showing what they are called in English and two other official languages.

1.3   Translation

1.3.1 Translate the extract from Article 21 quoted in the Chapter ("Every citizen of the Union may write …") into another official language. Then find the official translation and compare it with your own. Which do you think was the original language? Does it show? Does it matter?

1.3.2 Translate one of the three common myths about multilingualism mentioned at the end of the chapter. Get your translation revised by a native speaker of the target language. Ask them to explain their suggested revision changes.

1.4   Tools

1.4.1 Use a graphics package or spreadsheet to illustrate how and when the official languages of the EU have increased from four to 11.

1.4.2 Use the Tables function of your word processing package to produce a simple table showing, in the first column, the 15 Member States, in the second column, their official languages, and (optional) in the third column, any other national or regional languages spoken in those countries.

1.5   Debate

1.5.1 "The EU could function with a single working language." Discuss the pros and cons.

1.5.2 "Current EU language policy is unfair to speakers of 'minority' languages such as Catalan and Welsh." Discuss.

2. The EU institutions – their roles and their translation services

People often use the expression "the EU" inaccurately, to mean "the EU institutions" ("I'd like to work as a translator with the EU" or "Those offices belong to the EU").

This reflects the common misconception that "the EU" is a single organisation, generally assumed to be large, amorphous, and located in Brussels. In fact there are several EU institutions, and they are not all in Brussels.

When used correctly, **"the EU"** stands for **"the European Union"** and refers to all the countries that belong to it. Together these countries make up the political entity called "the EU". If you mean "the EU institutions", it is better to say that – even if it is less snappy.

The workings of the EU institutions are generally misunderstood – partly because they are complicated, and partly because they keep changing. The institutions are evolving as the EU grows and the Member States agree on new areas of cooperation. This is confusing for the detached observer. But if you want to work for the EU institutions or translate material about them, you must understand the basics.

This chapter describes, very briefly, what the institutions do and how they deal with translation. We describe the present situation, after the entry into force of the Treaty of Amsterdam on 1 May 1999. For a more detailed account of the institutions' activities and historical development, readers should consult the Europa server (http://europa.eu.int). There are also many special publications and leaflets available at EU Info Points throughout Europe.

How the EU institutions interact

The European Union is managed by the EU institutions:
- the democratically elected European Parliament;
- the Council, which represents the Member States;
- the Commission, guardian of the Treaties, endowed with powers to initiate and execute Community legislation;
- the Court of Justice, which arbitrates on Community law;
- the Court of Auditors, which monitors finances;
- the European Central Bank, which supervises economic and monetary union and the euro;
- and finally, the consultative bodies involved in economic, social and regional matters (Economic and Social Committee and Committee of the Regions) and the European Investment Bank, which finances economic development.

In a nutshell: the Commission **proposes**, the Parliament and the Council **decide.** The two Committees (Economic and Social Committee and Committee of the Regions) **advise**. The Court of Justice **issues rulings** on the interpretation and application of European Community law. The Court of Auditors **checks** how the EU Budget is spent.

In trying to understand the workings of the EU institutions, it is helpful to remember that the name of each institution is somewhat confusingly used to refer both to the core political body and to its administrative departments. Thus "the Commission" can refer either to the 20 Members of the Commission or to the several thousand staff who keep the institution running. This can be misleading in statements such as "Tony Blair advocated reducing the size of the Commission" as reported in the UK national press in October 2000. It is important to know whether he was referring to the Members of the Commission or to the Commission staff. (In fact he was referring to the former, after enlargement. In his speech to the Polish Stock Exchange in Warsaw on 6 October 2000, he said: "In the long run, I do not believe that a Commission of up to 30 members will be workable. The present intergovernmental conference must and will address the size of the Commission. More radical reform is not possible this time round in view of the worries of some states. I simply give my view that, in the end, we shall have to revisit this issue and streamline considerably.") (http://www.fco.gov.uk/news/speechtext.asp?4215).

The names of the EU institutions are often misused, even in the quality press, and they are easily confused with other bodies that have similar names (European Council and Council of Europe, etc.). Some of the most common problems are mentioned below, in the sections on each institution.

The eight major European institutions and bodies have a total of 28 876 permanent posts (see *General Budget of the EU* for 2000, "Staff" section). The largest is the European Commission, with 20 862 permanent posts. Far from being the vast army of officials decried by the Eurosceptic press, the European Commission is a relatively small organisation, bearing in mind that the European Union has 374 million citizens with 11 official languages. The local authority for any medium-sized provincial town employs more people. The numbers employed by central government are far larger: the British Civil Service has 22 times as many staff as the European Commission (460 000 civil servants in Whitehall, according to *The Times*, 30 September 1999:12).

Just under one fifth of the institutions' staff work in the translation and interpretation services, as professional linguists (translators, interpreters, terminologists, and lawyer linguists) and as secretaries and other support staff. As explained in Chapter 1, many texts have to be published in all the official languages. The meetings to prepare and finalise those texts involve delegates who may speak any of these languages. The public are entitled to understand what the EU institutions are doing, and of course to address them (in speech and in writing) in any of the official languages.

Translators deal with the written word, translating documents, while interpreters deal with the spoken word, translating speech. The two jobs are never combined in the EU institutions, as there is more than enough work to keep all the translators and interpreters busy; but in some cases, linguists do transfer from translating to interpreting and *vice versa*.

It is commonly assumed that there is a single "EU translation service" for all the institutions. That is not the case. In all, as described below, there are nine separate translation services attached to the various institutions and bodies of the EU. Naturally the translation services work together to create economies of scale where possible, for example, in organising recruitment and in accessing terminology. But each institution has specialised needs and ways of working, and if you want to translate well, you must understand the context. So each institution of any size has its own translation service. The smaller institutions and bodies share their translation services.

Interpreting is organised differently, in completely separate departments. The largest is the Joint Interpreting and Conference Service, which is part of the European Commission but provides interpreters and allocates meeting rooms for all the institutions except the European Parliament and the Court of Justice. The latter have their own, separate interpreting services. In the following section, we give details of the translation services but not of interpreting arrangements.

The next few pages explain the function and composition of the main institutions and bodies, where they are located, how they organise translation, and how to refer to them correctly. The number of translators in each section refers to the number of in-house translators in January 2000. The percentage of workload sent to freelance refers to the percentage of total workload in 1999. After the descriptions of the institutions and bodies, there is a brief section on the various Treaties and the concept of the "three pillars of the European Union". In an afterthought at the end of the chapter, we try to explain why, despite its complexity, the European Union does serve a useful purpose.

The European Parliament

Function:
The European Parliament's primary objectives are like those of any Parliament – to pass good laws and to scrutinise and control the use of executive power. It shares budgetary authority with the Council of the European Union and can therefore influence EU spending; the Members of the European Commission cannot be appointed without its approval, and it has the power to dismiss them (collectively, not individually) by passing a motion of censure. Its responsibilities have been gradually widened and its powers strengthened. It is the largest multinational parliament in the world.

Composition:
It has 626 members, from all 15 Member States, representing all of the EU's major political currents. It is directly elected by the 374 million citizens of the EU every five years.

Location: The European Parliament meets both in Brussels and in Strasbourg. Its Secretariat is in Luxembourg, where it was originally established in the 1950s. At that time there were no facilities in Luxembourg for holding plenary sessions in four languages. The first plenary session was therefore held in Strasbourg, an *ad hoc* solution which the French Government defended until in 1992 the Council confirmed that Parliament should have its seat in Strasbourg; that plenary sessions should be held there; and that some part-sessions should be held in Brussels. For reasons of proximity to the other institutions, the parliamentary committees meet in Brussels. That is why the European Parliament can also be described as peripatetic.

Translation service: Approximately 410 in-house translators (full-time equivalent), all in Luxembourg. In 1999 about 28% of its workload was sent to freelance translators and agencies. All the European Parliament's debates are translated into the 11 official languages by freelances (in 11 translation agencies) and published on its website.
The European Parliament also has in-house translators in its Minutes Division and a small group of lawyer-linguists (translators with legal qualifications) in its Legal Service.

Official name:
The European Parliament.
Less formal alternative: It may be referred to simply as "Parliament" (no definite article), as long as there is no risk of confusion with national parliaments.
It is no longer correct to say "The Assembly". This title was used in the past and may be found in old texts.

The Council of the European Union

Function:
The Council of the European Union is the forum in which the Member States legislate for the Union, set its political objectives, coordinate their national policies and resolve differences between themselves and with other institutions. In the Council, the representatives of the governments of the 15 Member States can assert their interests and try to reach compromises.

Composition:
The Council is composed of one national minister from each Member State (or a representative at ministerial level). Which national ministers attend each Council meeting will depend on the subject discussed (an Agriculture Council will bring together national ministers of agriculture, for example). Council members are empowered to commit their government and are politically accountable to their national parliaments.

The Council "Presidency" (the right to chair the Council) rotates between the Member States at six-monthly intervals.

The European Council brings together the Heads of State or Government of the Member States and the President of the Commission, to review policy guidelines, achievements and plans. Also referred to as "summits", European Councils take place at least twice a year, usually towards the end of each Presidency, in one of the major cities of the Member State holding the Presidency. At the European Council held in Nice, France, in December 2000, it was decided that from a certain time on (not specified) European Councils would be held in Brussels.

Location: The General Secretariat of the Council is in Brussels. The Ministers may meet anywhere.

Translation service: Approximately 640 in-house translators, all in Brussels. Freelance translation is very rare (about 0.25% of total workload in 1999) and is channelled through the Translation Centre in Luxembourg. The Council also has a small group of lawyer-linguists (translators with legal qualifications, also called legal/linguistic experts) in its Legal Service.

Official name:
The Council of the European Union.

Less formal alternatives: The Council of Ministers, the Council. The Latin name "Consilium" is used on nameplates and in letterheads and electronic addresses.

It is no longer correct to say "the Council of the European Communities"; see the section on the "three pillars" of the EU for an explanation.

Frequently confused with:
The European Council, which is not the same thing; see above.

The Council of Europe, which is a different organisation, not an EU institution, and based in Strasbourg, France.

The European Commission

Function:
The European Commission has several distinct functions:
• It has the right to initiate draft legislation and therefore presents legislative proposals to the European Parliament and the Council. The major decisions on important legislation are then taken by the ministers of the Member States in the Council, usually in codecision with the European Parliament.
• As the Union's executive body, it is responsible for implementing the European legislation, budget and programmes adopted by Parliament and the Council.
• It acts as guardian of the Treaties and, together with the Court of Justice, ensures that Community law is properly applied. It can institute legal proceedings against Member States which fail to implement EU directives.
• It represents the Union on the international stage and negotiates on behalf of the whole EU in international trade relationships.
Composition:
At present there are 20 Members of the Commission (or "Commissioners"), at least one from each of the Member States, appointed for a five-year term. The President is appointed by the Member States' governments after consulting the European Parliament. Members of the Commission are obliged to be completely independent of their national governments and to act only in the interests of the European Union.

Location: Brussels and Luxembourg (as well as several other locations throughout Europe).
Translation service: Approximately 1300 in-house translators, two thirds in Brussels and one third in Luxembourg. The Commission's Translation Service has small field offices (2 translators) in most European capitals, attached to the Commission's Representation there. It sends about 20% of its workload to freelance translators and agencies.
The Commission also has a small group of lawyer-linguists (translators with legal qualifications) in its Legal Service.

Official name (in legislation and formal contexts):
The Commission of the European Communities.
Less formal alternatives: The European Commission (now preferred in most other contexts) or the Commission.
The name may refer to either:
– the political body formed by the 20 Commissioners, also referred to as "the College of Commissioners" – a Gallicism, but a convenient one; or
– the administrative departments, also referred to as "the Commission departments".

> **It is not correct** to say "Commission of the European Union", "Commission of the EU", or "EU Commission"; see the section on the "three pillars" of the EU for an explanation.
> **Sometimes confused with:** the European Commission of Human Rights (a different body, not an EU institution, located in Strasbourg, now defunct); the Economic Commission for Europe (a United Nations body).

The European Court of Justice

> **Function:**
> The Court of Justice provides the judicial safeguards necessary to ensure that the law is observed in the interpretation and application of the Treaties and in all of the activities of the Union. Its judges must ensure that Community law is not interpreted and applied differently in each Member State. It has jurisdiction to hear disputes to which the Member States, the Community institutions, companies and individuals may be parties.
> **Composition:**
> 15 judges and 8 advocates general, appointed for a renewable term of six years.

> **Location:** Luxembourg
> **Translation service:** Approximately 230 in-house translators, all in Luxembourg. Court of Justice translators must have legal qualifications and are referred to as "lawyer-linguists" and "legal revisers". The Court of Justice sends about 12% of its workload to freelance translators and agencies.

> **Official name**:
> The Court of Justice of the European Communities (CJEC)
> **Shorter alternatives:** the European Court of Justice (ECJ) or the Court of Justice.
> Only use the expression "the European Court" or " the Court" if there is no danger of confusion with another Court (see below).
> The Latin name "Curia" is used in the Court's logo, on nameplates and in letterheads and electronic addresses.
> **It is not correct** to say "the EU Court".
> **Frequently confused with:**
> The European Court of Human Rights in Strasbourg
> The International Court of Justice in The Hague.

The Court of First Instance

Function:
The Court of First Instance was set up to relieve the Court of Justice of part of its workload (allowing it to concentrate on its central tasks of ensuring the uniform interpretation of Community law) and to protect individuals' rights by providing a two-tier judicial review system closer to that of the Member States. It deals with cases brought by individuals or companies (e.g. certain types of competition cases, staff disputes). Its judgments are subject to appeal to the Court of Justice.

Location: Luxembourg
Translation service: The Court of First Instance and the European Court of Justice share the same translation service (and all other services).

Official name:
The Court of First Instance (French: *le Tribunal de première instance*).
It is not correct to say "the Tribunal" (a Gallicism used by some writers).

The European Court of Auditors

Function:
The Court of Auditors' main function is to monitor the European Union's finances and point out areas where their management needs to be improved. In so doing, it functions as the European Union's external auditor.
The Court of Auditors is required by the EC Treaty to assist the European Parliament and the Council of the European Union in exercising their powers of control over the use of the budget. It produces an Annual Report for the previous financial year and this Report is a key factor in the European Parliament's decision on whether or not to approve past spending and release the future budget.
The Treaty on European Union added a new element to the Court of Auditors' tasks. It is now required to provide the Council and Parliament with a Statement of Assurance as to the reliability of the accounts and the legality and regularity of the underlying transactions.
The Court may also submit its own observations on specific issues by way of Special Reports, sometimes covering several financial years.
Composition: There are 15 members, appointed for a renewable term of six years.

Location: Luxembourg
Translation service: Approximately 62 in-house translators, all based in Luxembourg. The Court of Auditors sends about 4.5% of its workload to freelance translators and agencies.

> **Official name**: The European Court of Auditors.
> **Shorter form:** The Court of Auditors. When the context permits, i.e. if there is no risk of confusion with the Court of Justice, the name may be shortened to "the Court".
> The Latin name "Curia Rationum" is used in the Court's letterhead, on nameplates and on the Court's neck-tie.

The following are not European Union **institutions**. Most of them are **bodies** (French: *organes*) of the European Union. They have an advisory or coordinating role laid down in the Treaties.

The European Central Bank

The European Central Bank has the power under the EU Treaty to adopt Regulations that are binding and directly applicable in the Member States, but it is not strictly speaking an EU institution or body.

> **Function:**
> The European Central Bank is the central bank of the euro area. It coordinates – with the national central banks of the Member States that have adopted the euro as their national currency – all relevant central-banking related activities.
> Its decision-making bodies are the Governing Council, the Executive Board and the General Council. For further information see the ECB's website (www.ecb.int).

> **Location:** Frankfurt
> **Translation service:** Approximately 30 in-house translators, all in Frankfurt. The ECB sends up to 75% of its workload to freelance translators and agencies.
> It also has a small group of lawyer-linguists assigned to the same organisational area as its translation service.
> The working language of the ECB is English. Its English translators are recruited as "translator/editors" and they spend up to 80% of their time editing English texts written by non-native speakers of English, to prepare the texts for publication and/or translation into the other official languages.

> **Official name**: The European Central Bank.
> **Shorter form:** Abbreviated to "ECB".

The European Ombudsman

Function:
Every citizen of each Member State is both a national and a European citizen. All European citizens have the right to apply to the European Ombudsman if they consider themselves victims of "maladministration" by the EU institutions or bodies, or if they feel they have been unfairly treated (for example, not accepted for recruitment). Corporate bodies can complain as well as individuals.
Composition: One person (the European Ombudsman).

Location: Strasbourg
Translation service: Provided by the European Parliament (see above).

The Economic and Social Committee

Function:
The Committee brings together representatives of the EU's trade unions, employers and social and professional groups to advise the Commission, the Council and the European Parliament on issues such as employment, operation of the single market and transport policy. It is consulted before the adoption of most Community decisions and may also issue opinions on its own initiative.
Composition: 222 members.

Location: Brussels
Translation service: Approximately 140 translators, working with those of the Committee of the Regions in the Joint Services (see below).

Official name: As above.
Shorter form: ESC; "Ecosoc" is used only in informal contexts.

The Committee of the Regions

Function:
The Committee of the Regions ensures that regional and local identities and prerogatives are respected, by involving representatives of regional and local bodies in the development and implementation of EU policies. It has to be consulted on matters concerning regional policy, the environment and education.
Composition: 222 members. Some are key figures in European political life: regional presidents, mayors of large cities and heads of local authorities.

> **Location:** Brussels
> **Translation service:** Approximately 58 translators, working with those of the Economic and Social Committee in the Joint Services (see below).

> **Official name**: As above.
> **Shorter form:** No known variants apart from the acronym "COR", which must be used with care.

Joint Services of the Economic and Social Committee and the Committee of the Regions

> **Function:** Provides administrative and logistic support for the Economic and Social Committee and the Committee of the Regions.

> **Location:** Brussels
> **Translation service**: Approximately 198 in-house translators (140 ESC translators and 58 COR translators, as indicated above), all in Brussels. Only 1% of the workload is sent to freelance translators and agencies.

The European Investment Bank

> **Function:**
> The European Investment Bank is the European Union's financing body. It finances investment projects which contribute to the integration and balanced development of the Union.

> **Location:** Luxembourg
> **Translation service:** Approximately 26 in-house translators, all in Luxembourg. About 30% of the workload is sent to freelance translators and agencies.

> **Official name**: As above.
> **Shorter form:** Abbreviated to "EIB".

Decentralised Community Agencies

Several Agencies, Foundations and Centres have been set up by decisions of the European Commission or one or other European Council, for specific tasks (some of which were previously carried out by Commission departments). They work as autonomous bodies. Most do not have translation services of their own. This list is not final; new agencies may be set up as the need arises.

European Agency for the Evaluation of Medicinal Products (EMEA), London
European Environment Agency (EEA), Copenhagen
European Training Foundation, Turin
European Centre for the Development of Vocational Training (CEDEFOP), Thessaloniki
European Monitoring Centre for Drugs and Drug Addiction (EMCDDA), Lisbon
European Foundation for the Improvement of Living and Working Conditions, Dublin
Office for Harmonisation in the Internal Market, Alicante
Community Plant Variety Office, Angers
European Agency for Safety and Health at Work, Bilbao
European Police Office (Europol), The Hague
European Monitoring Centre on Racism and Xenophobia, Vienna
Translation Centre for the Bodies of the European Union, Luxembourg

The Translation Centre

Function:
The Translation Centre was set up in 1994 to provide the translation service for a large number of European agencies and bodies. In 1995 the Council enlarged the role of the Centre, allowing it to work for institutions and bodies that have their own translation services, and charging it with a central role in interinstitutional cooperation on translation-related matters.
The Translation Centre has its own financial resources, constituted by transfers from the agencies and institutions in exchange for the services it provides.

Location: Luxembourg
Translation service: The Centre currently employs some 65 in-house translators, all in Luxembourg. Most of the translators are employed on renewable temporary contracts. About 50% of the Centre's workload is sent to freelance translators and agencies.

Official name:
The Translation Centre for the Bodies of the European Union.

The Treaties

Over the years, the three "European Communities" (one of which was the "European Economic Community") have evolved into a single "European Community" and then into the "European Union". This section explains why. The political motivation behind these changes came from the Member States' acceptance of closer integration and their desire to cooperate (or otherwise) in certain areas of common interest.

The first three treaties set up three separate "European Communities":

Place and date signed (entry into force)	Full title	Short title
Paris, 18 April 1951 (same date)	Treaty establishing the European Coal and Steel Community	Treaty of Paris; ECSC Treaty
Rome, 25 March 1957 (1 January 1958)	Treaty establishing the European Atomic Energy Community	Euratom Treaty; the *other* Treaty of Rome
Rome, 25 March 1957 (1 January 1958)	Treaty establishing the European Economic Community	*The* Treaty of Rome, EEC Treaty; EC Treaty

Adapted from Kennedy 1998:343ff.

The three Communities were the European Coal and Steel Community (ECSC), the European Atomic Energy Community (EURATOM) and the European Economic Community (EEC). Each Community had its own advisory, executive and administrative bodies. In 1967 these were merged:

Brussels, 8 April 1965 (1 July 1967)	Treaty establishing a Single Council and a Single Commission of the European Communities	Merger Treaty

Adapted from Kennedy 1998:343ff.

The next major Treaties ushered in important political changes but also a trend towards the name "European Community " (confirmed in Article G.1 of the Maastricht Treaty) and finally, the creation of the "European Union" by the Maastricht Treaty:

Place and date signed (entry into force)	Full title	Short title
Luxembourg, 17 February 1986 and the Hague, 28 February 1986 (1 July 1987)	Single European Act	The same, or SEA
Maastricht, 7 February 1992 (1 November 1993)	Treaty on European Union	TEU; The Treaty of Maastricht; the Maastricht Treaty
Amsterdam, 2 October 1997 (1 May 1999)	Treaty of Amsterdam amending the Treaty on European Union, the Treaties establishing the European Communities and certain related acts	Treaty of Amsterdam

Above table adapted from Kennedy 1998:343ff.

Nice, 26 February 2001	Treaty of Nice amending the Treaty on European Union, the Treaties establishing the European Communities and certain related acts	Treaty of Nice

The "three pillars" of the European Union

The abbreviations EC and EU are not synonymous. **EC** (European Community) activities are those coming under the "first pillar" (see below); **EU** (European Union) activities cover much wider areas of international cooperation.

The three pillars were originally created by the Treaty of Maastricht, which entered into force on 1 November 1993. In effect the second and third pillars were new areas of EU cooperation supplementing the "European Community" areas that already existed. It is important to understand that the second and third pillar affairs (the common foreign and security policy, and justice and home affairs) do not fall within the jurisdiction of the European Community and are therefore not administered by the European Commission, since they are considered to be key areas of national sovereignty.

Some elements of the third pillar were transferred to the first pillar by the Treaty of Amsterdam, which entered into force on 1 May 1999.

The European Union			
First pillar: **The European Community** (former EEC + ECSC + EURATOM, now EC)	**Second pillar:** **Common foreign and security policy**	**Third pillar:** **Justice and home affairs**	
Common policies (agricultural, commercial, social, environment, etc.)	**Common defence WEU (Western European Union)**	• Asylum policy • Control on external borders • Immigration	transferred to first pillar by Treaty of Amsterdam
Economic and monetary union (EMU)	**Foreign and security policy**	**Europol (European Police Office)**	
Citizenship of the Union			
	(Common strategies added to second pillar by Treaty of Amsterdam)		

How this affects the *names* of the EU institutions:

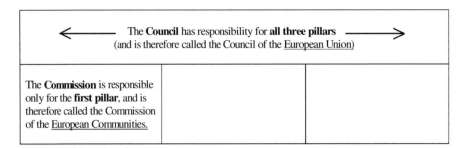

The **Council** has responsibility for **all three pillars**
(and is therefore called the Council of the <u>European Union</u>)

The **Commission** is responsible only for the **first pillar**, and is therefore called the Commission of the <u>European Communities.</u>

An afterthought

The EU institutions are often criticised for their complexity and intricate structure. In their defence, there are two things one can say:

- First, the European edifice was conceived by committees and modified in deals hammered out by politicians. Its makers were only human. Building Europe entails surrendering blocks of sovereignty, but politicians are not willing to surrender sovereignty – or at least, they are not willing to be seen to surrender it. Many criticisms are justified, and we pro-Europeans sincerely hope that something can be done to make the workings of the EU institutions understandable and relevant to the people of Europe.
- Second, and more important, despite all justified and unjustified criticisms, the EU is achieving the main purpose of its founders, which was to secure peace, prosperity and mutual respect for its Member States. Anyone who belittles this achievement is advised to have a chat with a member of Europe's older generation who has experienced world war at first hand and

has survived the pain, deprivation and persecution that accompanied it ... not forgetting those who didn't survive.

Having at least fifteen different nationalities working alongside each other is difficult, but the difficulties are not insuperable. In the institutions, which are a microcosm of Western Europe, we tend to overlook this achievement too. Recently an American visitor, Peter Mulrean from the US State Department, summed it up perfectly in an interview with our staff magazine. He had spent a year on an exchange programme working for the Commission and he talked about the insight he had gained into the European Union – and the new knowledge he would take back to his normal job in the US. Then he was asked what he would most miss about the Commission. His reply:

> "An experience that I will miss is riding the elevator, especially up to the 15th floor in the Charlemagne building. You stand there and you hear a couple of Spaniards speaking here and a Swede and a Dane there switching easily into English and French to talk together. And then they go their separate ways and work together. And that was what Schuman and the others had in mind. The Commission more than any other body represents that. Coming from a country that prides itself on being a melting pot, I find that you are the great melting pot, and that is a great accomplishment and strength. You forget that after a while: it is wonderful that it can become normal to work together with all your different backgrounds and languages and ways of working." (*Commission en direct* 137, 16 - 22 September 1999:8)

Exercises for students

2.   The EU institutions

2.1   Research
2.1.1   Visit the Europa website (**http://europa.eu.int**) and read more about the institutions. Find out which EU institutions or bodies have NOT been mentioned in this chapter.

2.1.2   Find out which country currently holds the Presidency of the Council. Which country will take over next?

2.2   Terminology
2.2.1   Make a three-language glossary of the names of the institutions mentioned in this chapter (hint: use Europa to find the names).

2.2.2   Using the information given in Chapter 2, produce a list in English showing the official names, acceptable shorter names, and incorrect names (where indicated), for the three main institutions and the Courts.

2.3   Translation

2.3.1   Visit the Europa website as in Exercise 2.1.1. Select a 300-word extract from one of the institution's sites in one of your foreign languages. Translate it into another official language (preferably your mother tongue). Then compare your translation with the official one. Which is better? Why?

2.3.2   Translate the last paragraph of this chapter into another language. How can you tell from Mr Mulrean's reply that he is an American? Can you convey that in your translation?

2.4   Tools

2.4.1   Taking the figures given in Chapter 2, use a graphics package to produce a graph or chart showing the number of translators in each EU institution/body and the percentage of translation sent to freelance.

2.4.2   Select a 300-word extract (preferably in your mother tongue) from one of the institution's websites on Europa. Copy and paste it into your word processing program. Edit it. Use a document comparison or track changes function to show the changes you have made.

2.5   Debate

2.5.1   Discuss how the structure and functions of the EU institutions compare with those of the institutions in your home country. Which EU institution has a law-making function comparable with that of your national parliament? (Hint: trick question)

2.5.2   "The EU institutions are irrelevant to the general public". Discuss. If you agree, suggest how they could be made more relevant.

3. How to get in

How to become an EU staff translator

People employed by the institutions reflect the cultural diversity of the Member States of the European Union. Staff are drawn from all the 15 Member States, and a few more besides. They must feel at ease in a multicultural and multilingual working environment away from their home country.

All permanent employees of the European Union institutions, including translators, have the status of "officials", or European civil servants. After an initial trial period, they are employed for life and cannot be dismissed without serious cause. Selection is therefore very stringent. To be eligible for appointment as an official, candidates must have the right level of qualifications and must pass exacting written and oral examinations.

Recruitment by open competitions

The majority of the European Union institutions and bodies recruit their in-house translation staff through **open competitive examinations** (referred to as "competitions" in this book, for the sake of simplicity).

Most of the institutions join forces and hold jointly organised or "interinstitutional" competitions. These typically involve the following institutions and bodies:
- European Parliament
- European Commission
- European Court of Auditors
- Economic and Social Committee
- Committee of the Regions.

The exceptions are the following:
- Council of the European Union
- European Court of Justice.

In view of their special requirements, these two institutions hold their own competitions, but the general requirements and procedures are similar to those described below.

Any institution can hold its own competitions if it has special recruitment needs that are not shared by the other institutions.

In the following EU-related bodies, the staff are not all European officials. Translators are recruited directly by separate recruitment procedures:

- European Central Bank, Frankfurt (http://www.ecb.int/)
- European Investment Bank, Luxembourg (http://eib.eu.int/)
- Translation Centre, Luxembourg (http://www.cdt.eu.int/).

Translators wishing to work for those bodies should contact them for details. Vacancies are advertised in the national press (according to the languages required) and on their websites, indicated above.

The EU institutions' recruitment competitions are held every few years to fill the vacancies arising for translators into a particular language (normally every three years for each language, although the interval is sometimes longer). They are announced in a notice published in the Official Journal and have an identification code starting with "EUR/LA/..." (if it is an interinstitutional competition) or "COM/LA/..." (if it is just for the Commission). They are advertised simultaneously in the national press of the country or countries concerned. Information is also sent to universities and translators' professional associations and to all individuals of the language concerned who have written asking for information since the previous competition for that language. Competitions for English-language translators are advertised in the United Kingdom and in Ireland, and internationally. All the institutions put recruitment information on their websites (accessible via http://europa.eu.int)

The actual competition consists of **written tests** (an eliminatory translation test and a series of multiple-choice questions on European Union matters and general knowledge, and two more translation tests, translating into the language of the competition from two official languages), followed at a later stage by an **oral test**. There may also be optional written examinations to test the successful candidates' ability to translate out of additional foreign languages. The competition takes eight to ten months on average, from the deadline for applications through to the oral tests. The names of all the successful candidates are placed on a **reserve list**. The entire procedure, from the first announcement of the competition to actual recruitment, takes a minimum of about 18 months. As with all other staff recruitment, having one's name on the reserve list is no guarantee of recruitment.

To fill immediate vacancies, the translation services select translators from the reserve list and invite them for further interviews and medical examinations. Those not called for interview, or called but not selected for appointment at this stage, may still be recruited later until recruiting from that list closes. The same applies to candidates who decline a post offered but ask for their name to be kept on the reserve list. The reserve lists are valid for about a year from the oral tests and may be extended for a further period.

The Commission's policy is to recruit translators at the **starting grades**, which are **LA8 (assistant translator)** or **LA7/6 (translator)**; some other institutions recruit directly at higher grades. **Assistant translators** are those who have no professional experience, or very little, and have graduated recently. **Translators**, on the other hand, are expected to have several years' full-time professional experience since graduation.

Whenever new Member States join the Union, limited numbers of translators and revisers are recruited at all levels, not just at the starting grades, to create the teams needed for translation into the new languages.

Success rates in recent translators' competitions

Standards required of candidates during the recruitment competitions are challenging. Only a small number of extremely able candidates is successful, varying from 1% to 10% of all applicants. Here are the overall results of some recent competitions.

Target language: Swedish
Interinstitutional competition held in 1995 (Lead institution: Commission)

Swedish translators LA7/6
Applications received:	244 (61 men + 183 women)
Accepted for written tests: :	175 (40 men + 135 women)
Passed oral and placed on reserve list:	27 (7 men + 20 women)

Swedish assistant translators LA8
Applications received:	293 (62 men + 231 women)
Accepted for written tests: :	253 (52 men + 201 women)
Passed oral and placed on reserve list:	22 (11 men + 11 women)

Target language: English
Interinstitutional competition held in 1996 (Lead institution: European Parliament)

English translators LA7/6
Applications received:	418 (130 men + 288 women)
Accepted for written tests: :	257 (90 men + 167women)
Passed oral and placed on reserve list:	29 (13 men + 16 women)

English assistant translators LA8
Applications received:	887 (212 men + 675 women)
Accepted for written tests: :	532 (144 men + 388 women)
Passed oral and placed on reserve list:	21 (13 men + 8 women)

Target language: French
Single-institution competition held in 1999 (Commission)

French translators LA7/6
Applications received: 1133 (357 men + 776 women)
Accepted for written tests: :   852 (273 men + 579 women)
Passed oral and placed on reserve list: 18 (8 men + 10 women)

French assistant translators LA8
Applications received: 1435 (319 men + 1116 women)
Accepted for written tests: :   1079 (252 men + 827 women)
Passed oral and placed on reserve list: 16 (7 men + 9 women)

General conditions of eligibility for competitions for translators or assistant translators

Nationality: Candidates must be citizens of a Member State of the European Union (or of a country that is about to become a Member State).

Qualifications: Candidates must hold a university degree or equivalent qualification, either in languages or in a specialised field (economics, law, science, etc).

Knowledge of languages: Candidates must have a perfect command of the target language (usually their mother tongue) and a thorough knowledge of at least two other official European Union languages. A knowledge of additional languages is an advantage. Translators translate exclusively into their mother tongue. However, in future recruitment exercises, especially for the new official languages, some institutions are considering including additional tests in translation out of the mother tongue into English or French.

Age: At present the upper age limit is 45 for LA 8 and LA 7 competitions.

Experience:
LA8: No experience is required for LA 8 competitions, but they are open only to candidates with a recent degree, obtained no more than three years before the competition is announced.
LA7: At least three years' experience is required for LA 7 competitions. The experience may be in translation or in some relevant professional field (economics, finance, administration, law, science, etc.).

A recruitment competition – from start to finish

1. Preparation

The translation service decides on its new recruitment needs and draws up a competition notice (*avis de concours*) together with the other institutions wishing to take part and their personnel departments. For interinstitutional competitions, one of the larger institutions is appointed "lead institution".

The competition notice is submitted for approval to a committee called the COPAR (*Commission paritaire*) if only one institution is involved, or the COPARCO (*Commission paritaire commune*) if it is an interinstitutional competition. It is then published in the Official Journal and in the press.

While this is in hand, the lead institution appoints the selection board (*jury de concours*) which will oversee the competition. The selection board consists of a chairman or chairwoman and an equal number of members representing the administration and the staff. The chairperson and members all have deputies, and the meetings are not quorate unless all three components – chairperson, administration side and staff side – are present.

The selection board's first task is to examine the applications received for the competition. The candidates' qualifications must be checked to ensure that they meet the conditions specified in the notice of competition. The check is based on the information supplied by candidates on the application form and in the supporting documents. Every applicant is informed in writing of the selection board's decision whether or not to admit them to the competition.

Applicants who believe that a mistake has been made in assessing their application may ask for it to be reconsidered. They should send a letter explaining why they think a mistake has been made, within 30 working days of the date of the postmark on the letter informing them that their application has not been accepted. The selection board reconsiders the application and notifies the candidate of its decision as soon as possible.

The selection board then prepares the various tests. New tests are created for every competition. The **multiple-choice questions** on general and EU knowledge are usually prepared in the working language of the selection board (English or French in most cases) and then translated into the language of the competition if that is different.

For the **translation tests**, the selection board chooses general texts in the EU official languages. This is not easy, because the texts must be of similar difficulty in all source languages and they must all be of the same length (25 lines or 45 lines depending on the test in question). The texts are always originals (never translations), and are usually taken from respected newspapers and periodicals known for their *gravitas* and language quality.

The selection board also decides how much time should be allowed for each test. Candidates are informed of this when they are invited to the competition. They are also informed whether or not they can use dictionaries (this varies according to the tests and/or the competition).

2. The tests

The venue
Depending on the availability of examination rooms and the place of origin of

candidates, the tests may be held in Brussels, Luxembourg, or some other convenient venue in the European Union (e.g. Athens, if it is a competition for Greek translators). If there are several examination centres, the tests are held at exactly the same time in all of them. Special arrangements are made for disabled candidates upon request.

Written tests

The written tests are always fully described in the notice of competition. They typically entail three *hand*written translation tests (sometimes without dictionaries) and a multiple-choice questionnaire to test general and EU knowledge. Applicants should not underestimate the level of knowledge required to pass the tests.

Marking

The test papers, *which do not bear candidates' names,* are marked by the members of the selection board and/or by any assessors who may have been appointed. Each paper is marked independently by at least two different people. It takes time to do this properly, and the members of the selection board also have other jobs to do, so some delays are inevitable before the results of the written tests are known. The work of the selection board is secret. Candidates should not attempt to contact the chairperson or members of the selection board, except via the complaints procedure specified in the notice of competition.

Applicants who get high enough marks in the written tests are invited to the oral tests.

Oral tests

These are usually held in Brussels or Luxembourg. The selection board asks questions about the European Union and other more general questions, aiming to assess the candidate's knowledge and general education, powers of expression, personality and aptitude for relations with other people. Most of the interview with the selection board is held in the candidate's mother tongue, although the tests of oral skills in other languages are naturally held in those languages.

3. The results of the competition and recruitment

Fairly soon after the oral tests, candidates are informed of the results of the competition. Successful candidates are placed on a **reserve list** (a list of all successful candidates). If the competition has been held to fill specific posts, the successful candidates will be recruited rapidly, but being on a reserve list does not guarantee an offer of employment. Reserve lists are normally valid for one year and can be extended for up to three years. Successful candidates will be informed of any extension of validity. They should keep the institution informed of any change of address or employment so that they can be contacted rapidly when a post falls vacant.

Failing a competition does not affect anyone's chances of being admitted to a subsequent one, and passing it.

How to work for the EU institutions as a freelance translator

The EU institutions use large numbers of freelance translators. Chapter 2 shows the percentage of workload sent to freelance by each translation service. The EU-wide rules on public procurement, laid down in Council Directive 92/50/ EEC, require public authorities to select their service providers by competitive tendering, and the EU institutions are in no way exempt from this requirement. Therefore, although it may be tedious and time-consuming for hard-pressed freelance translators to prepare formal tenders and collect all the necessary documentation, they must complete these formalities if they want to work for us. And unfortunately they must go through the process again every few years. This is because the market changes: new translators may join the market, and we have to give newcomers a chance to bid for freelance work. Free-lance rates may also change and we are required to take these developments into account.

An inevitable consequence of competitive tendering is that we do not pay uniform rates to our freelance translators. In their tenders they name their price and if they are otherwise acceptable, that is the price we pay. As a result, the freelance rates we pay per page (1 page = 1500 characters or approximately 300 words) vary from €25 in Italy to €65 in Denmark, reflecting the national differ-ences in tax, social security and insurance obligations for freelance translators.

The tendering procedure is complicated for freelance translators; but it is complicated for the EU institutions too. For that reason we try, wherever possi-ble, to cooperate with other institutions and bodies so we can share the preparatory work involved and the freelance lists that result. (For some comments on this point, see the section on Interinstitutional Cooperation at the end of Chapter 6).

The lists of approved freelance contractors include translators into all the official languages and they cover various subject specialisations. The language combinations and specialisations required are always indicated in the call for tenders published in the Supplement to the Official Journal and displayed on the institutions' websites.

Calls for tender

Calls for tender may differ in terms of the language combinations required, the institutions involved and subject areas covered; it is only possible to give very general information here. Tenderers must read the particular tender notice very carefully and follow the instructions given there, however peculiar they may seem (for example, it is compulsory to submit tenders in two sealed envelopes, one inside the other).

Some of the specialisations (known as "sub-lots") for which freelance tenders have been invited in recent years are:

- General and political matters, publications for the general public
- Specialised legal texts
- Financial, economic and monetary matters, insurance
- Competition law, public procurement, fight against fraud
- Agriculture and fisheries
- Regional policy, structural funds
- External relations, EU enlargement, trade
- Development aid and humanitarian aid
- Science and technology
- Telecommunications, IT
- Environment
- Chemistry, biochemistry and biology
- Medicine, pharmacology
- Transport
- Social affairs and employment
- Culture and heritage
- Education, training, youth
- Statistics and mathematics

Types of contractor eligible

Usually both individuals and companies may apply. They must be declared and working officially, operating in accordance with the law. Companies must be officially registered in the European Economic Area. The full requirements are always given in the tender notices. Some EU institutions and bodies (the Commission and the Translation Centre) accept tenders from both companies and individuals; both are welcome to apply and are used for freelance work. Companies offer larger capacity, but individuals offer more even quality and lower rates. Recently, the European Parliament has expressed a preference for companies or "groupings" of individuals able to cover a wide range of source languages. Some innovative individual freelances have created groupings to meet Parliament's requirements and have reported that (somewhat to their surprise) teamwork does have some advantages over isolation!

The two stages of a call for tender

In the first stage of the procedure, we first check that bids meet the formal criteria set out for the presentation of tenders. Tenders are then examined in the light of a set of previously announced **selection criteria** (compliance with social security and tax obligations, for example). In the second stage, the final choice is made on the basis of **award criteria**, which are a combination of price and quality. Quality is determined initially by the tenderer's description of their translation methods and quality control procedures.

Individual translators and agencies submitting successful tenders sign **framework contracts** with the European Commission. Framework contracts are usually valid for three years, after which they may be extended with an index-linked price adjustment.

Prices must be quoted in euros and they are binding – no bonuses can be paid for urgent or difficult work. Within the framework contract, the freelance translator or company receives an individual contract for each piece of work.

Dynamic ranking

The position of each translator or company on the approved list for each specialisation, and hence their chance of receiving work, is determined by a combination of price and quality. The quality of every job is evaluated and the ranking may be altered – either once a year (for some institutions' lists) or after every job (for others).

Language combinations not covered by calls for tender

For some language combinations, demand is very low and it is not justifiable to organise calls for tender – for us, they generate administrative costs, and for freelance translators, they generate expectations that would be disappointed. So for those language combinations that are not (or not yet) covered by a call for tenders, including translations out of and into non-official languages, the institutions use an *ad hoc* procedure: bids are invited from at least three freelance translators for the job in question, usually by fax, and the contract is awarded on the basis of the selection criteria used in calls for tender. Translators who already have a framework contract for another source language are approached first; if that is unsuccessful, we approach translators on the "waiting list" (see the end of this section).

Freelance translation in practice: the steps involved

1. **Decision** to send text to a freelance translator (see Chapter 6, In-house or freelance?)

2. **Selection** of a contractor from the list, based on four criteria:
     the language combination
     the subject area

the ranking of the contractor (by price/quality ratio)
the availability of the contractor

The language combination and subject area are entered in the in-house data-base, which displays a list of names in order of price-quality ratio. The translation unit or freelance coordinator responsible contacts the freelance individuals or companies, by phone, fax or e-mail, in order of ranking, until they find one willing to accept the job. The selection is confirmed and the contract is drawn up by the freelance unit. The contract (or "order form" as it is known in in-house parlance) is handled exclusively by the freelance unit; the translation units are not authorised to deal with contractual formalities or to discuss prices (or complaints about late payments!)

3. Assistance to freelance translators
In addition to the source text and reference documents, usually sent by e-mail, freelance translators should be given information on the purpose of translation and the name of the freelance coordinator responsible for that job, or another contact person or terminologist who can help them.

4. Translation
Before approaching the contact person or terminologist about translation prob-lems, freelance translators should if possible try all the usual sources of information (Internet, dictionaries, Eurodicautom, CELEX or EUR-lex). A dim view is taken of freelance translators who just translate all the easy bits and then present us with a list of unsolved problems!

Formatting is important; unless otherwise instructed, the format of the trans-lation should exactly match that of the original.

5. Returning the finished translation
The deadline is imperative unless an extension has been granted (which is rare). The translation should be returned by e-mail as instructed. The invoice should be sent to the appropriate freelance translation unit by post.

6. Quality control
The institutions have a contractual obligation to evaluate the quality of all free-lance translations. This "evaluation" may range from full revision to a spot-check that everything is there. The choice will depend on the purpose and importance of the translation and on our past experience with that freelance translator. When new freelance translators are used, we always revise at least five pages of their first translation. All this has to be done rapidly, so we can give the green light for payment. The institutions have strict instructions to minimise late payment

(there is an official limit of 60 days). The evaluation is also tantamount to a "mark" (out of 10) for that translation. It is entered in the database and will affect the translator's future ranking.

Positive evaluation (mark of 7-10/10):
Payment is made with 60 days of invoice.

Negative evaluation (mark of 0-6/10):
The translator is informed that a second evaluation is required. This is handled by the Interinstitutional Committee for freelance quality evaluation, which has representatives from the Commission, Parliament and the Translation Centre. The Committee decides what further action should be taken (types of action, in ascending order of gravity: zero, warning letter, cancellation of framework contract for a particular subject area or language combination).

7. Feedback
We know we should send detailed feedback, but time does not always permit it. We apologise unreservedly to all freelance translators for this failing.

Rapid post-editing by freelance post-editors

The Commission's Translation Service arranges for rapid post-editing of machine translation (known as "PER" from its French name: Post-Édition Rapide) by freelance translators working into English, French or German out of those three languages. Here again, the contractors are selected from a list of freelance translators and companies who have tendered for this type of work in a special call for tenders. The rates charged are lower than for full translation (averaging about 50%), reflecting the fact that the text is pre-translated – after a fashion – and the translation quality requirements are lower than for full translation. Speed is far more important. PER users are willing to accept lower quality in return for speed, and the service is suitable for urgent and ephemeral texts translated solely for information (not for publication).

The "waiting list" for freelance translators

Even if you have just missed a call for tenders, or have only just heard about the system, it is worth sending your name and CV to the EU institutions, preferably directly to the freelance translation unit, to register your interest in working for them as a freelance translator. As mentioned above, they may offer you work if you translate out of or into a language that is not covered by the calls for tender. In any case they will inform you when the next call for tenders for your target language(s) is published.

How to get placements and other help with translator training

Paid and unpaid placements for students and recent graduates

Each institution has its own arrangements for student and graduate placements. The European Parliament's "Translator Training" site (http://www.europarl.eu.int/stages/reg2_en.htm) gives the most complete information on placements, traineeships and scholarships. It has links to the other institutions' sites on this topic and to application forms.

Trainees are accepted in all departments, not only in the translation services.

The European Commission's Translation Service offers five-month in-house traineeships for graduates who wish to acquire an understanding of its work and gain professional translation experience.

Those selected are assigned to a translation unit comprising translators of the same mother tongue. Trainees do the same work as their staff colleagues, translating into their mother tongue from at least two other official languages. Their work is revised by experienced senior staff. Some trainees are assigned to a language library or to the terminology unit or other support unit in the Translation Service.

Trainees receive a grant of approximately €700 per month, plus a family allowance for married trainees. Some unpaid traineeships are also available.

Paid traineeships at the Commission run for five months starting on 1 March and 1 October. The deadlines for submitting applications are 30 September for the traineeship period starting in March and 31 March for the one starting in October.

Unfortunately, demand far outstrips the small number of traineeships available each year and the EU institutions have to turn down many applicants.

For people wishing to apply for a traineeship, there are four basic requirements. They must
- hold a full university degree;
- be below 30 years of age;
- be able to translate into their mother tongue from two of the EU's official languages;
- not have completed a traineeship in another European Union institution or body.

They should fill in and return the special application form available online at http://europa.eu.int/comm/translation/en/form.pdf. The application will be considered when the next series of traineeships for translators is organised, and applicants will be notified if they are selected.

Study visits are unpaid placements for undergraduates, usually for four weeks at the time most convenient for the student and the institution. They are available only to students whose university has a made a general arrangement with the European Commission or another institution to "place" students whose university course requires them to spend some time on practical work in an organisation or company.

Cooperation with universities training translators

Cooperation with universities takes many forms. Every translator comes from a university, and many maintain links with their *alma mater*, even returning to teach or lecture on an informal or semi-formal basis. Speakers from the institutions (the Directors-General and Directors of the translation services, the language coordinators at the Commission and Parliament, and other staff) are occasionally invited to speak at universities and academic conferences, and thus build up contacts.

In return, university teachers and lecturers often come to speak and give seminars at the EU institutions, as part of the in-house training provided for translators. They are also welcome to visit Brussels and Luxembourg with groups of student translators, for a guided tour of the service. These group visits must be arranged a few months in advance, and we cannot cover any of the group's expenses – all we can offer is our time, to describe our work and show the visitors a typical translation unit, a presentation of our translation aids such as EC-Systran, and goodwill. This provides an opportunity to get to know the practical context of translation work. Some other contacts with the world of Translation Studies are presented on the "Translation Theory" section of the Commission Translation Service's website (http://europa. eu.int/comm/translation/theory).

"Visiting EU translator" project
The "visiting EU translator" project (DE: "EU-Gastübersetzer"; FR: "traducteur invité") was originally proposed by Tampere University, Finland, in November 1996. Since then a number of successful visits to various universities have taken place. Visiting EU translators spend approximately six weeks at a university, teaching and receiving training. They teach translation into their mother tongue and give lectures on translation in the EU institutions; in exchange they can attend lectures and classes to perfect their knowledge of the foreign language in question. They should already have a sound knowledge of that language.

The main visible benefits for the visiting translators are that they receive a depth of exposure to the language that is not possible on standard language courses, and establish useful contacts. There are also less obvious benefits: the experience of teaching, the opportunity to project the reality of the EU institutions, and a few weeks away from the constant pressure of translation work – perhaps under a different kind of pressure – enabling them to return refreshed. In the Commission, the project is restricted to two or three translators per year, and they must have the right profile (language knowledge of the right level, and preferably some teaching experience). The motivation is definitely not to "preach EU methods" (there are none that we know of) but simply to build bridges between academic circles and the EU institutions' translation services.

The initial invitation must come from the host university, specifying the most convenient dates for the translator's visit and the mother tongue required. It should be sent to the Director-General, European Commission Translation Service, 200 rue de la Loi, B-1040 Brussels, for the attention of the Language Coordinator responsible for the country where the university is located.

If there are several equally suitable candidates, the choice can be made by the host university (based on the CVs of applicants, e-mail contacts, etc.).

There are no payments to or from the host university. Visiting translators pay most of their own expenses. If the university can provide cheap accommodation, it is appreciated.

A final idea: translators as guinea pigs
It is surprisingly rare for serious researchers to use the 2000 in-house translators in Brussels and Luxembourg, and our 1000 freelance colleagues, for research into human translation or as a testing ground for new theories. We are occasionally contacted by postgraduate students writing dissertations and theses, but the subject of study is usually fairly limited, and we rarely see the results. Researchers who can design projects that will not disrupt production are very welcome to contact us with proposals. Projects likely to enhance production are, of course, especially welcome.

Exercises for students

3.   How to get in

3.1   Research
3.1.1 Find out which EU institutions and bodies offer information for freelance translators on their websites (don't forget the Translation Centre).
3.1.2 Find out when the next recruitment competitions for translators are to be held, and for which target languages.

3.2   Terminology
3.2.1 Select 10 terms used in this chapter in connection with the recruitment of in-house translators, and find the equivalents in two other official lan-

guages. Produce a three-language glossary with a definition of the English term.

3.2.2 Make a small "Public Procurement" glossary in three languages, using terms drawn from Council Directive 92/50/EEC.

3.3 Translation

3.3.1 In your **first foreign language**, write a letter and CV applying for freelance work or a work placement with an EU institution, or appealing against a decision that goes against you in some way – rejection, etc. Ask a fellow-student to translate it into your mother tongue. Are you happy with the translation? Is it what you would have written yourself?

3.3.2 Take an extract from European Parliament's "Translator Training" website (http://www.europarl.eu.int/stages/) and do either one of the following exercises:

a) Translate it into another official language, without consulting the official translation on the website. Then compare the official translation with your own. Which is better?

b) Re-write it in a more appealing way.

3.4 Tools

3.4.1 Check all the figures given on the page headed "**Success rates in recent translators' competitions**". Do the numbers of men and women add up to the total? (Sorry, translators have to check these points too!)

3.4.2 Convert these figures into a pie chart or bar chart comparing the figures for the three target languages mentioned.

3.5 Debate

3.5.1 Discuss possible research projects that could use the EU institutions' translators as guinea pigs.

3.5.2 If in-house translators were not recruited by competitive examinations as described in this chapter, what other recruitment methods could be used? Might other methods be fairer on applicants, or yield more satisfactory results for the employer?

4. What we translate

What do we translate? Almost anything, it seems at times. Once we tried to think of a subject we had *not* dealt with in a translation. Knitting? (No – clothing manufacture.) Football? (No – free movement of footballers.) Sex? (No – sexually transmitted diseases, harmonisation of condom size, employment status of prostitutes, pornographic content of television without frontiers, etc.) But in the vast universe of translation, our little planet is dominated by political, legal and economic topics. These make up the bulk of our work.

The analysis that follows is not based on a pre-existing official classification. It is an attempt to explain the purpose and context of translation work in the institutions of the European Union. It shows the panorama as viewed from the European Commission, but includes many texts translated in the other institutions.

1. Treaties

The European Union is essentially a political creation, so we should first mention the basic political texts that define its character, its aims and its ambitions: the Treaties. Starting out from the founding Treaties establishing the ECSC, the EEC and Euratom, and moving on by way of the Single European Act, we have recently arrived at the Treaties of Maastricht, Amsterdam and Nice, all of which have added new layers of democracy to the basic structures, and new social and economic dimensions, such as the single currency.

These Treaties are drawn up at Conferences of the Member States (Intergovernmental Conferences or IGCs) with input from the Commission, national governments and civil society. Once the Treaties have entered into force, it is the Commission's job to ensure they are implemented; but before that, they must be ratified by the national parliaments and published in all the official languages, which means that each language version is accepted by all the Member States. Translating the Treaties is the most crucial translation activity of all. It is carried out by the translators at the Council of the European Union. It is crucial because it will have an impact on all the subsequent work of translators.

It is in the Treaties that things get their names: the institutions, the types of legal instrument, the underlying principles of the Union (freedom of movement, the single market, subsidiarity, etc.) and its decision-making procedures. These names create a legal precedent and must therefore be used consistently. For example, when the United Kingdom and Ireland joined, it was the Treaties that named the entities they joined the *European Communities* rather than the *European Commonwealth*. Later, it was the Treaty that fixed the name *European Central Bank* rather than *Bank of Europe*. It is on the basis of these texts that words such as *Directive* or *Regulation* enter the legal vocabulary of the Member States with a special meaning that they never had in the dictionaries.

This text category also includes the *Accession Treaties / Acts of Accession* signed by Member States and countries joining the EU. New Member States usually bring new languages into the fold, and each new language will be designated by the Act of Accession as an official language of the EU. This status will be confirmed by the simultaneous publication of the Treaties in the new language, with a legal force identical to all the existing language versions.

And because the new language becomes an official language of equal validity, the countries that are already members of the EU have the right to express doubts or reservations during the accession negotiations about certain terms used in the new language version of the Treaty. Again, it is the Council that has the major responsibility of translating these texts.

The *Conclusions of the European Council* is another key political document, also translated by the Council translators. These Conclusions set out the political guidelines issued by the European Councils that are held twice a year and attended by the Heads of State or Government of the Member States.

2. Legislation involving several institutions

The staple diet of translators in the European Union institutions is *legislative texts* and *legislation-related texts*. The European Union is different from other major international organisations such as the United Nations in the following ways:
- the Member States have agreed to pool their sovereignty in certain areas;
- the EU institutions produce **laws**;
- together these make up a body of law that takes precedence over national law in each Member State;
- the Court of Justice has to ensure that they are correctly applied by courts throughout the EU.

It is fair to ask why we still use the terms *directive, regulation* and so on, instead of simply referring to *laws*. This has in fact been suggested at recent intergovernmental conferences. But invariably the Member States' representatives decided that they prefer to keep to the traditional names. This terminology may be good for tradition and legal accuracy, but it is not good for openness and communication. Members of the public know perfectly well what a *law* is, but as a rule they don't know what a *Council directive* or *regulation* is. This is one of the most flagrant instances of Eurospeak hindering communication by (deliberately?) camouflaging the political and legal nature of the EU institutions.

The European Commission is the only institution that has the "right of initiative": that is, the right to propose new legislation. Although the Commission can decide independently to table a draft law, it rarely does so without prompting from elsewhere. It systematically receives suggestions and instructions from the Council, the European Parliament, the Member States and civil society. Often the instructions they issue are very specific (for example, a food-poisoning incident or a ferry disaster may generate demand for a directive on food safety standards or international sea transport). It is often in response to a request from one of these parties that the Commission will start looking at a problem and then launch the lengthy process of drafting, consultation and re-drafting that will culminate in the adoption of legislation by the Council and the European Parliament.

Here are some examples of draft legislation translated in 2000. The name of the Commission department or **Directorate-General** (DG) responsible for drawing up the proposal is given in brackets after the title in each case (see the Europa server for details of the Directorates-General in the Commission and other institutions):

Proposal for a Directive of the European Parliament and of the Council on the promotion of electricity from renewable energy sources in the internal electricity market (Energy)

Proposal for a Council Regulation listing the third countries whose nationals must be in possession of visas when crossing the external borders and those whose nationals are exempt from that requirement (Justice and Home Affairs)

Proposal for a Regulation of the European Parliament and of the Council on action by Member States concerning public service requirements and the award of public service contracts in passenger transport by rail, road and inland waterways (Transport)

Proposal for a Regulation of the European Parliament and of the Council laying down detailed rules for the organisation of official controls on products of animal origin intended for human consumption (Health and Consumer Protection)

Proposal for a Directive of the European Parliament and of the Council on universal service and users' rights relating to electronic communications networks and services (Information Society)

The titles are given in English here, but English is not necessarily the original language. In fact – and this greatly influences the day-to-day work of translators – it is often impossible to determine the "original" language of a text.

A legislative proposal may start life as a paper by an EU official (the single currency, the euro, was first proposed 30 years before its adoption in a paper by the Luxembourger Pierre Werner, who was a senior Commission official at the time) and such papers may be written in German, although French and English are more usual. The text may have gone through several successive versions in English, and some of these will have been translated into all the official languages, but when it comes to be discussed by the College of Commissioners, the final amendments may be made in French, to the French version. The choice of "working language" will be pragmatic, and will depend on the languages used by the officials responsible, departmental tradition or habit within the drafting unit, and the language knowledge of the Commissioner who will have to defend the proposal.

The few titles listed above, and those that follow, will illustrate the extreme variety of topics covered and the fields in which translators for the institutions must be able to ply their trade and demonstrate their translation ability. They also give some idea of the distinct style of language that has come to be used in Community legislation. This is often different from the style and traditions of national legislation, so as to avoid favouring any particular legal or national culture and to create a style and a tradition specific to the European Union, in all official languages.

This means that new translators starting work in an EU institution must realise that they are entering what is almost a different culture, and certainly a different tradition. They must be prepared to bring some humility to the task, for the following reasons:

- because what we translate may already have been translated before, in an earlier version – not only once, but several times over;
- because there are conventions that specify one particular translation option (and not necessarily the one you consider the most correct, the most elegant or the most apt) rather than all the other possible ones;
- because you are now a mere link in the long chain of the legislative production process;
- because the translation you are producing, after passing through various linguistic, legal and political filters, will one day be published in the Official Journal of the European Union. And there, it will not be presented as a translation, but as an *original*, an authentic piece of Community legislation, with a legal force identical to that of all the other language versions.

For all these reasons, when you translate for the EU institutions, you are not the master of your text. And don't imagine that translators are on a par with legislators, just because they are part of the legislative process!

In point of fact, much of the legislative work of the EU institutions is a permanent process of updating the legislation in force, as in the following examples:

Proposal for a Council Regulation amending Regulation (EC) No 2742/1999 fixing for 2000 the fishing opportunities and associated conditions for certain fish stocks and groups of fish stocks, applicable in Community waters and, for Community vessels, in waters where limitations in catch are required and amending Regulation (EC) No 66/98 (Fisheries)

Proposal for a Directive of the European Parliament and of the Council amending Directive 76/207/EEC on the implementation of the principle of equal treatment for men and women as regards access to employment, vocational training and promotion, and working conditions (Employment and Social Affairs)

The Commission's translators are the first to be involved in the translation of draft legislation, as we shall see shortly. But as most draft legislation has to be submitted to the European Parliament and the Council, the translators there have to translate the various series of amendments proposed by those institutions before the draft can be finalised and adopted by the Council (or adopted jointly by the European Parliament and the Council under the codecision procedure).

In turn, the translators working for the Economic and Social Committee and the Committee of the Regions have to translate the opinions of those bodies on the draft legislation proposed by the Commission.

When we reach this stage, the translation work rarely entails "technical" difficulties because of the lengthy gestation of the draft and the preparatory work that has gone before. It will be more a matter of choosing the right legal terms, checking on the correct use of standard formulae, and adhering to the agreed terminology for that field.

What makes these texts difficult to process is their tortuous progress, involving several different services and several different political levels, generating several successive versions and repeated translation of nuances and details whose point is often obscure. It is not unusual for the same legislative text to return five or even ten times for translation, sometimes even more. New technology has helped us to save time by identifying exactly which passages have been amended, inserted or deleted in the basic text (manual marking of amendments was always notoriously unreliable).

3. The preparatory stages

Even before the Commission can present a draft law to the Council and the

Parliament, there is a great deal of preparatory work to be done, often starting by wide-ranging consultation of economic and social circles and national ministries, by inviting comments on a *Green Paper:*

Green Paper on greenhouse gas emissions trading [sic] *within the European Union* (Environment/Energy/Enterprise)

The Commission may also indicate areas where it does not (or does not yet) wish to produce legislation, but where it would like to open a political debate, coordinate action by the Member States, or test the ground with the other institutions:

Communication from the Commission to the Council, the European Parliament and the Economic and Social Committee. Integrating environment and sustainable development into economic and development cooperation policy: Elements of a comprehensive strategy (Development)

Communication from the Commission to the Council, the European Parliament, the Economic and Social Committee and the Committee of the Regions. A Commission communication on communications strategy in the last phases of the completion of EMU (Economic and Financial Affairs)

Communication from the Commission to the Council and the European Parliament. The Organisation and Management of the Internet: International and European Policy Issues 1998-2000 (Information Society)

Communication from the Commission to the Council and the European Parliament, the Economic and Social Committee and the Committee of the Regions. A strategy to improve the operation of the VAT system within the context of the internal market (Taxation)

Communication from the Commission: e-Learning – Designing tomorrow's education (Education and Culture)

A draft law is usually preceded by a study or series of studies commissioned by the Directorate General responsible, and then by preliminary draft regulations or directives that will be widely discussed (often for several years in some areas, such as taxation) by committees of representatives from the Member States. These working documents account for a large proportion of the translation work at the Commission. Here are some examples of preparatory texts:

Upgrading the Investment Services Directive (93/22/EEC) (Internal Market)

Commission White Paper on Environmental Liability (Internal Market, Insurance Committee).

The departments of the Commission are constantly producing studies, memoranda, drafts, communications and policy papers on all the subjects it has to deal with. These may ultimately give rise to draft legislation, or serve as reminders or suggestions for the Member States.

Often it is with these preparatory texts that translators experience the greatest difficulties, for two reasons:

- firstly, because the authors do not have time to draft preparatory documents with all the care they would give to a legislative proposal, and in any case the texts are often drafted in French or English by Commission staff or outside consultants who are not writing in their mother tongue;
- secondly, given the "exploratory" nature of these texts, translators often come up against the difficulty of finding established and universally acceptable terms in their language for products or concepts that are new or not even fully developed.

It can be a problem, for example, for languages other than English to find terms for new developments in information technology or financial services; and for all languages there are problems coining terms for new political concepts. The concepts of **subsidiarity** and **cohesion** are important for the European Union, but difficult to express clearly in non-Romance languages. The concept of **governance,** a key feature of modern political theory in the era of globalisation, which is being taken very seriously in current work at the European Commission, has no obvious translation in several official languages.

So translators are forced to innovate, preferably in agreement with authorities and colleagues in their home countries. One day they may even have the pleasure of reading their freshly minted neologism on the front page of their national newspaper.

4. Legislation issued by a single institution ("autonomous instruments")

Not only does the Commission act as an **initiator**, with the right to initiate legislation under the conditions described above, but it also acts as an **executor** of common policies and programmes. In other words it has the duty to run the common policies of the EU (competition policy, agricultural policy, fisheries policy and trade policy) and the multi-annual programmes (research framework programme, assistance to non-member countries, humanitarian aid programmes, etc.).

Like the other institutions, the Commission also has to run itself (personnel matters and internal administration), and all institutions have the right to issue "autonomous instruments" (French: *actes autonomes*) for this purpose. Resolutions and Opinions by the European Parliament and the Economic and Social Committee are also autonomous.

In the Commission, most but not all of this work is done by issuing its own **Commission** Regulations, Directives and Decisions. Here are some examples:

Commission Regulation establishing the standard input values for determining the entry prices of certain fruit and vegetables (Agriculture)

Commission Regulation fixing Community producer and import prices for carnations and roses with a view to the application of the arrangement governing imports of certain floricultural products originating in Cyprus, Israel, Jordan, Morocco and the West Bank and the Gaza Strip (Agriculture, Trade)

Commission Regulation implementing Council Regulation (EC) No 577/98 on the organisation of a labour force sample survey in the Community concerning the specifications of the 2001 ad hoc module on length and patterns of working time (Employment and Social Affairs)

Commission Decision amending Decision 97/404/EC of 23 July 1997 setting up a Scientific Steering Committee and Decision 97/579/EC of 23 July 1997 setting up scientific committees in the area of consumer health and food safety (Health and Consumer Protection)

Commission Regulation imposing a provisional anti-dumping duty on imports of polyester staple fibres originating in India and the Republic of Korea (Trade)

These texts account for a considerable proportion of the translators' work in some parts of the Commission's translation service, because here too there is a great deal of preparatory work at the early stages. But much of it is routine work, based on standard models for some of the texts and with well-established terminology in most of the areas concerned.

There is another field in which the Commission has special executive powers assigned to it by the Treaty, and that is **competition**. The Commission's activities in this area are subject to very specific procedures and tight deadlines and deal with matters of vital interest to economic operators throughout the world (such as the Commission action against Boeing, the American aircraft manufacturer, in 1988). This generates a considerable volume of high-priority and often highly specialised translation work for the Commission's translators:

Commission Decision relating to a proceeding under Article 85 of the EC Treaty and Article 53 of the EEE Agreement (Case Fujitsu – AMD Semiconductor)

Commission Decision relating to a proceeding under Article 85 of the EC Treaty (Case Volkswagen)

These harmless-sounding titles refer to two important decisions taken after thorough investigations and after consulting the Advisory Committee on Restrictive Practices and Dominant Positions, which includes representatives from all the Member States.

In the first case, the Commission decided that it should not contest the joint venture agreement between Fujitsu and AMD, two world producers of semiconductors, one Japanese and the other American. In the second case, which received a lot of attention in the press, the Commission condemned the commercial practices in Italy of the German car manufacturer Volkswagen, and concluded, after 48 pages of technical and legal justification in the Official Journal, that "In view of the gravity of the infringement a fine of ECU 102 million is imposed on VW AG".

One special aspect of these competition decisions is that they are addressed to named firms, business associations, etc. and the authentic text in each case is the one in the language or languages of the recipients; the other translations are for information only.

5. Political scrutiny

The essential checks and balances to the legal powers of the EU and the executive role of the Commission are provided by various mechanisms for democratic surveillance and accountability. This surveillance is exercised to some extent by the Commission itself, which has to monitor the Member States' implementation of EU law and the transposition of EC Directives into national law. But a leading role is played by the European Parliament, through its various committees and plenary meetings, and by the Council. Together the European Parliament and the Council keep a close watch on the way the Commission manages the policies and programmes under its control, and the way it disburses the EU Budget. The latter type of scrutiny is based primarily on the Reports of the Court of Auditors; for translators in that institution, translating the lengthy and detailed annual reports and special reports of the Court of Auditors is a major part of the workload.

When the Council and Parliament adopt a piece of legislation, they frequently include in it an obligation for the Commission to submit regular reports on the implementation of the provisions in question:

Second report from the Commission to the Council on the situation in world shipbuilding (Competition/Enterprises/Trade)

19th Report from the Commission to the Council on the implementation in 1995-96 of Regulation (EEC) No 3820/85 on the harmonisation of certain social legislation relating to road transport (Employment)

Report from the Commission to the Council and the European Parliament relating to the implementation of Council Decision 98/729/EC amending Decision 97/256/EC so as to extend the Community guarantee granted to the European Investment Bank to cover loans for projects in Bosnia and Herzegovina (Budget)

Report of the Commission on the application of Directive 79/409/EEC on the conservation of wild birds. Update for 1993-1995 based on information supplied by the Member States on the application of national measures adopted pursuant to the Directive (Environment).

A classic form of parliamentary scrutiny is the practice of addressing *parliamentary questions* to Members of the Commission. These may be *oral questions*, in which case they are dealt with by the interpreters (although briefing notes and defensive points, pre-empting likely questions, may have to be prepared in advance and translated into the language of the Commissioner, and the questions and answers have to be published) or they may be *written questions*. The translation services of the European Parliament and the Commission have to deal with hundreds and possibly thousands of these questions every year – although activity reaches a peak in the run-up to the European elections!

This helps to show why there are differences between the translation workload (in terms of language range) of the different institutions:

- In the European Parliament, all MEPs submit their written questions in their own language. The European Parliament must therefore have the resources needed to translate out of all the official languages and into all the official languages, including rare combinations such as Greek into Finnish, or Danish into Portuguese. (They can of course fall back on relay translation via a "pivot language" in emergencies.) The same conditions hold at the Economic and Social Committee and the Committee of the Regions, where representatives meet from both sides of industry, and from local and regional authorities, and all must have the right to speak in their national language.
- In the other institutions, documents are usually written in English and French, so translators working into other languages find themselves mainly translating out of those two languages. The situation is quite different for the English and French translators in those institutions: they have to translate texts written in a much wider range of source languages. This is because they translate

(often for internal information) texts written by government officials in the Member States, by representatives of civil society, and by ordinary members of the public exercising their basic right to communicate with the EU institutions in their own language. This difference in the "diet" of translators is illustrated at the end of this chapter.

The parliamentary questions and answers may of course deal with any subject of interest to an MEP or their constituents, and they may be subjects far beyond the usual activities of the EU institutions. But on the whole they are short and relevant texts, including the following answer, which may have set a record for concision in an EU document:

> "No."

One can only hope that all the different language versions said the same – mistakes are always possible ...

6. Judicial scrutiny

The European Court of Justice is responsible for interpreting and applying European Union law (starting with the Treaties, also known as "primary legislation") by way of its judgments and rulings. Thus the Court is a driving force of European integration, because it protects the rights of Europe's citizens, confirms the primacy of EU law over national law, and ensures that EU law is uniformly interpreted and applied by courts throughout the Member States.

As explained in Chapter 2, the Court has its own translation service, staffed by highly specialised translators who are all lawyers by training. They have to tackle an ever-increasing workload. Cases may be brought before the Court in any of the official languages (even Irish, which is an official language at the Court of Justice) and all documents have to be translated into French, which is the internal working language of the Court. The **Court's judgments and orders** are translated into the language in which the case was brought and will become the sole authentic version. They are also translated into all the other languages for information. In addition the **opinions of the Advocates General**, which they draft in their own language, have to be translated too. To provide information for national governments on the interpretation of EC law, **requests for preliminary rulings** are also translated into all languages and notified to each government.

The **European Court Reports** (French: *Recueil de la jurisprudence*) are the equivalent, in the legal area, of the Official Journal of the EU. They are published in all the official languages. Today they constitute a corpus of case law of a size comparable with the corpus of Community legislation in force.

As explained in Chapter 7, when a new country joins the EU, the Community *legislation in force* has to be translated and published in full in the language of that country so that it can apply immediately in the new Member State; but the *case law* is no longer translated in full, because the judgments often relate to legislation that is no longer in force. Only the most important judgments are translated into the new country's language – but even these add up to tens of thousands of pages – and it may take several years of painstaking work.

7. Public scrutiny and administration

Texts that have to be translated in the institutions to allow public scrutiny of their work, and day-to-day administration, include:
- speeches to be delivered by leading members of the institutions;
- the debates of the European Parliament (translated by freelance agencies);
- minutes of the many committees that assist the Commission in its legislative and management functions;
- daily press releases;
- petitions to the European Parliament from members of the public;
- conference proceedings;
- correspondence with national ministries and the public (including e-mail).

Sample titles in this area:

Minutes of Committee on Maritime Fisheries sector (Employment)

Press release: Scientific Steering Committee adopts opinion on scientific justification of national BSE measures (Public Health and Consumer Protection)

Proceedings of the Conference on "45 years of ECSC Social Research" (Employment)

8. Information for the public

Finally, there is an extremely important sector accounting for a large share of the workload in some translation teams:
- publications for the general public;
- websites and information databases.

The great challenge for translators of information booklets, databases and websites is to detach themselves from the administrative terminology and officialese they are required to use in legislative and quasi-legislative texts, and to write in a more reader-friendly and attractive style. This is not easy; and, as explained elsewhere in this book, the best efforts may be undermined by officials outside the translation service (misguided authors, interventionist proof-readers or careless typesetters). Many translators, too, tend to lapse into a robotic style and forget how important it is to see things from their readers' point of view.

Sample titles in this area of work:

Guidance on work-related stress – Spice of life or kiss of death?

The Community provisions on social security – Your rights when moving within the European Union

"Citizens First" information database (now on-line at http://europa.eu.int/scadplus/citizens/ and http://europa.eu.int/europedirect/)

"EUR-OP News" (free newssheet distributed throughout Europe by the Office for Official Publications; reviews recent EU policy developments and presents new publications).

* * *

"We never translate alone!"

Translators in the EU institutions must not expect excitement or drama; almost every day, they will have some jobs that are repetitive and boring. But if they can keep an enquiring mind and a positive attitude, they will come to understand the bigger picture of EU activity and to enjoy being part of it. For translators interested in learning languages, understanding other nationalities and immersing themselves in new and sometimes abstruse subject areas, the EU institutions provide unparalleled opportunities.

In-house and freelance translators working for the EU institutions should forget any idea of individual power or putting a personal imprint (or even their name) on their translations. In all but a few exceptional cases: when we translate here, we are members of a team. The team includes:

- precedent (the ghosts of translators past);
- revisers, who will alter, correct and sometimes even improve our translations;
- legal revisers who will further amend legislative texts to make them legally watertight;
- and of course the politicians, officials and others who will have their say on both style and substance in the course of the codecision procedure.

Codecision is the procedure whereby the "interinstitutional triangle" of the Commission, European Parliament and Council all have their say in legislative proposals. On average it entails 31 steps by 11 different services in the three main institutions. Only six of those steps involve the translation services.

A brief guide to Community legislation

1. Types of instrument

Because so much of our work is related to legislation, translators should understand the basic principles. As explained in Chapter 1, the three main forms of Community legislation (regulations, directives and decisions) are set out in Article 249 of the EC Treaty, which we quote again here, for the reader's convenience:

> A ***regulation*** *shall have general application. It shall be binding in its entirety and directly applicable in all Member States.*
>
> A ***directive*** *shall be binding, as to the result to be achieved, upon each Member State to which it is addressed, but shall leave to the national authorities the choice of form and methods.*
>
> A ***decision*** *shall be binding in its entirety upon those to whom it is addressed.*

Because **regulations** are binding in their entirety and applicable throughout the European Union, they are used in specific areas such as agriculture, customs and state aids. The Council often delegates power to the Commission to issue regulations on policies once it has adopted the overall framework and orientation (in instruments referred to as "framework regulations"). The most common example is Commission regulations on the day-to-day running of the agricultural policy; some other examples are given in Section 4 above.

Decisions are also directly binding, but only on those to whom they are addressed, and they must be notified to those persons before they can take effect. Sometimes they are addressed to the institutions themselves and concern administration and the setting-up of committees; some other examples are given above, relating to competition and aid policy.

Directives are a common type of Community legislation, perhaps because they are less intrusive. Looking again at the Treaty quotation above, we see that directives are *"binding, as to the result to be achieved"* – that is, they lay down general objectives. But they *"leave to the national authorities the choice of form and methods"* – that is, the national parliament or other authorities must adopt their own national laws and regulations to achieve those objectives. This process is known as **transposing** the directive into national law.

In his highly recommended book *Learning European Law*, Tom Kennedy says:

> "Often the end product of lengthy and tortuous negotiations, replete with compromises and fudges, [directives] represent, nonetheless, the collective will of the Member States to achieve certain objectives, usually laying

down a time within which those objectives must be attained." (Kennedy
1999, p. 114)

We translators know all about those compromises and fudges, and the difficulty
of replicating them with just the right flavour of fudge in all the official languages. But disregard our groans – there is an important point to be made about
the language of directives. They represent an **international compromise**, not
an edict from Brussels, as is so often claimed in the Eurosceptic press. Because
they are a **compromise**, they may contain some woolly phrasing (how else would
one reach a compromise?) and because they are **international**, they expressly
avoid using legal terminology that belongs to any particular national legal system. Directives are written in the language of the Community's common legal
culture, rooted in the Treaties and the secondary legislation derived from the
Treaties. When the various language versions are produced, they must be exactly similar in form and content, otherwise the parties to the compromise may
fear they have been swindled. So it is quite inappropriate to criticise them because they don't look or sound "natural". They will in any case be "translated"
into the national legal idiom when they are transposed into national law. In the
process, their form may change almost beyond recognition.

Recently, a group of translators at the European Parliament carried out a
study (not yet published) to compare Community directives with the national
legislation transposing them into law. They wanted to find out which was clearer
and more readable: the directive, or the national law? The results showed a very
wide range of outcomes. Some national laws were clearer (Sweden came out
top of the clarity league), but the majority of national transposing laws were
more obfuscatory than the directive upon which they were based.

Example 1:
The Italian version of Council Directive 88/378/EEC on the safety of toys
(Official Journal L 187/88:1-13) uses the word *bambini* (children), but in the
Italian national law (Decreto legge 27.9.1991, n. 313) it became *minori* (mi-
nors). No doubt there are good legal reasons for this change, but *bambini*
(children) is more readily understood by the general public, not to mention the
toy-owning public.

Example 2:
The Directive on consumer protection in respect of contracts negotiated away
from business premises (Council Directive 85/277/EEC) was implemented in
the United Kingdom by the Consumer Protection (Cancellation of Contracts
Concluded away from Business Premises) Regulations 1987 (SI 1987/2117).
Where the Community Directive refers to *doorstep selling,* the UK national
legislation prefers *contracts made at the doorstep*, no doubt for good legal rea-

sons, but not in order to make the law clearer to the average citizen.

(Note on the binding force of Directives: Lawyers would no doubt expect us to add that Directives *can* become directly binding in their original form under certain circumstances: if a Member State fails to transpose a directive into national law by the agreed date, or does so incorrectly.)

2. The anatomy of an instrument (cf. Regulation No 1, quoted in Chapter 1)

- Every instrument starts, after the title, with the name of the **enacting authority** (the Council, the Commission, or the Parliament and the Council).
- Then comes a series of phrases starting with the words "Having regard to ..." These are called the **citations** and they set out the legal basis of the instrument. Nothing can be done without a secure legal basis in the Treaties.
- After that there are a series of paragraphs introduced by the word "Whereas" in English ("*Considérant*" in French). These are called the **recitals** and they set out various policy considerations and the general justification for the instrument.
- Then comes a sentence in capital letters of the type: "HAS ADOPTED THIS REGULATION:" which names the **type of instrument** (a regulation in this case).
- Only then, finally, do we get to the Articles, which set out the **substantive provisions** of the instrument.

It is of course essential, for reasons of legal precedent and validity, that the phrases and terms used in these legal formulae are always translated in the same way.

A footnote: Language range

In most institutions (the exceptions are the European Parliament, the Economic and Social Committee and the Committee of the Regions) the range of languages translated by English and French translators is quite different from that of translators working into the other languages. Many incoming translations – written in the Member States and sent to the institutions – are translated only into English or French, for information. This makes for a much wider variety of languages in the "diet" of French and English translators. The texts translated into other languages are mainly outgoing texts, written in-house in English or French.

So, for example, the number of pages translated into English in the European Commission, in 2000, looked like this:

Language codes:

DA = Danish, DE = German, EN = English, EL = Greek, ES = Spanish, FI = Finnish, FR = French, IT = Italian, NL = Dutch, PT = Portuguese, SV = Swedish

Source languages for English translators:

DA 5099	DE 19287	EL 5513	ES 6480	FI 4846	FR 65673	IT 7619	NL 7569	PT 3072	SV 6186

Total pages translated into English from the other 10 official languages: 131 344 pages
Other source languages in addition (21 in all, not shown above): 2427 pages
Grand total translated into English in 2000: 133 771 pages

Whereas for the Danish translators, the pages per language were as follows (and the situation is very similar, *mutatis mutandis*, for those translating into Dutch, Finnish, Greek, Italian, Portuguese, Spanish and Swedish):

Source languages for Danish translators:

DE 1539	EL 80	EN 53609	ES 442	FI 61	FR 32489	IT 755	NL 211	PT 160	SV 72

Total pages translated into Danish from the other 10 official languages: 89 418 pages
Other source languages in addition (not shown above): 7 pages
Grand total translated into Danish in 2000: 89 425 pages

Exercises for students

4.   What we translate

4.1   Research
4.1.1. Find the full text of one of the items of draft legislation mentioned under heading 2 of this chapter, in two official languages.
4.1.2. Find out where Parliamentary Questions and answers (mentioned under heading 5 of this chapter) are shown on the Internet. Print out some questions and answers on the subject of multilingualism.

4.2   Terminology
4.2.1 What is *"greenhouse gas emissions trading within the European Union"* (mentioned under heading 3 of this chapter)? Find out what it means and what the equivalents are in all 11 official languages.
4.2.2 Make a small glossary of the terms used in the section on the anatomy of an instrument under the heading "A Brief Guide to Community Legislation" in this chapter. Give a definition (in your own words, or those used above) and the equivalent terms in two other official languages. Indicate the sources used.

4.3 Translation

4.3.1 Translate the title *Guidance on work-related stress – Spice of life or kiss of death?* (mentioned under heading 8 above) into another official language and/or explain why it cannot be translated.

4.3.2 Find a fairly short legislative proposal from the list mentioned under heading 2 above (perhaps the same one as you identified for Exercise 4.1.1). Without consulting the official translation, do your own translation, preferably from French or English into your mother tongue. Compare your version with the official version and decide which is better. Why?

4.4 Tools

4.4.1 Use presentation software such as PowerPoint to show how a Directive can be broken down into the elements mentioned in the section on the anatomy of an instrument under the heading "A Brief Guide to Community Legislation" in this chapter. You may either use a real Directive (but choose a short one, or shorten it), or invent a spoof Directive with the right structure and register.

4.4.2 Taking the figures given at the end of this chapter ("A footnote: Language range"), use graphics software to produce a more attractive presentation (bar chart or piechart).

4.5 Debate

4.5.1 It could be argued that international political compromises are not a good basis for national law. Re-read the paragraph starting with the quotation from Tom Kennedy above, and then say what *you* think.

4.5.2 In this chapter we say that "new translators starting work in an EU institution must be prepared to bring some humility to the task". But the authors of this book are old translators, so we would say that, wouldn't we? Do *you* agree? What are the implications?

5. Problems

Untranslatability

The Spanish philosopher José Ortega y Gasset pointed out in his essay *The Misery and Splendour of Translation*, written in the late 1930s, that there is not a one-to-one relationship between languages or between the cultures to which they belong. So any translation remains "an impossible venture" (*un propósito imposible*). And yet, paradoxically, that very impossibility is what encourages us to translate. In so doing we realise that the end result will never be quite the same as the text we started out with. Hence there is a utopian element in the labour of translation, just as there is, according to Ortega y Gasset, in any human endeavour worthy of the name.

The German philosopher Martin Heidegger claimed that translation could be damaging, in that it could pervert the sense of the original text. Criticising the translation of Ancient Greek philosophy into Latin, he wrote "Mit dieser lateinischen Übersetzung wird aber schon der ursprüngliche Gehalt des griechischen Wortes [...] abgedrängt, die eigentliche philosophische Nenn-kraft des griechischen Wortes zerstört" (1954:10). We must conclude that if translation is so destructive, Heidegger would have been happier if his own writings had been left untranslated (as here). But without translation, would Heidegger have had as much influence? Would it be fair if only readers of German had access to his writing, like a privileged secret society? Those questions may seem superficial; but they are not. They underlie the need for translation in international relations: the right to be heard, and to hear what others are saying, regardless of the language used; and, in the EU, the equal rights of all Member States and all European citizens to exert influence and have access to information.

Those of us who struggle daily with the miseries and splendours of translation are acutely aware that it is sometimes impossible and frequently approximate. But we will not abandon the endeavour. This chapter presents some of the difficulties we encounter when translating for the EU institutions.

Non-transferability of concepts

Some concepts are difficult to express in different languages for the simple reason that they are specific to certain countries for reasons of geography or climate. For example, the Mediterranean countries have a rich vocabulary of terms related to olive growing. Finland, Sweden and Denmark have no climatic chance of growing olives themselves, and little tradition of trade in olives. Yet EU directives and reports on olive-growing have to be translated into Finnish,

Swedish and Danish. This is not a ridiculous waste of money and effort, as Eurosceptics might claim: it is a legal obligation, as explained in Chapter 1 and Chapter 7. Farmers in the Nordic countries are entitled to know just what subsidies, bonuses and other benefits their Mediterranean counterparts may be getting (or not getting) under EU agricultural policy. Similar considerations apply to fishing in the Baltic, coalmining in Germany (several EU countries have no coal mines) and tolerated child labour (newspaper boys) in the United Kingdom and Denmark. These and many other activities will inevitably be mentioned in the reports, surveys and legislation that we translate in the EU institutions. How do we cope? By conscientious research and, if all else fails, by paraphrase.

Example: **The *"bâteliers"* problem**
The original six Member States – France, Germany, Italy and the Benelux countries: Belgium, the Netherlands and Luxembourg – had much legislation at EU level (the "EEC level" at the time) relating to navigation on inland waterways, because many of them were linked by the Rhine and major canals. But as new countries joined – Denmark, the UK, Greece, Spain and Portugal, which had never used inland waterways for international transport, or had abandoned them – some stilted and rather antiquated terminological equivalents were found, such as "EN: boatmen" for "FR: *bâteliers*", etc.

Translations full of archaic terms will not read very well, but they have to be produced if no more catchy and current terms exist.

Example: **Atlantic fish in Greek**
One ingenious solution, which is accurate but not reader-friendly (unless the reader is a biologist), is the use of Latin species names when there is no national equivalent. This was and still is necessary when legislation referring to Atlantic fish species has to be translated into Greek, as Greek has no names for certain non-Mediterranean species.

Similar but thornier problems arise when translating texts about the Member States' institutions and their educational, legal and social security systems. Do you translate "Chambre des députés" as "House of Commons" or "Bundestag"? No, of course not – it's not the same thing. But if you call it the "French lower house", the meaning may be unclear to some readers, and if you say "the lower house in the French parliamentary system" you may be accused of prolixity. In some contexts (depending on the target readers), it may be better to translate it as "the French equivalent of the House of Commons" or to leave it in French, with an explanation in brackets: the "Chambre des députés (French Parliament)".

Supranational concepts and Eurospeak

When translating texts about legal concepts recommended or imposed at

European level – consumer guarantees or paid maternity leave, for example – it may be misleading to translate the generic term by the "correct" specific term used at national level, even if an exact equivalent exists. When our translations are checked and rewritten by the author departments and lawyer-linguists of the institutions, national terminology may be replaced by the hated Eurospeak. The lawyers' explanation is as follows: using a correct but nationally specific term could lead to confusion; a supranational term which has no immediate national "meaning" may be preferable. This is because the text is about a single supranational concept, not the national equivalent (or rather: 15 slightly different national equivalents, one for each of the 15 Member States).

As explained in Chapter 4, much EU legislation is in the form of directives, which set out the general principles that have been agreed on by the Member States. Once directives have been adopted, they always have to be **transposed** into national law by each Member State. At that stage the generic Eurospeak concept (as translated by us and published in the Official Journal) is converted into a specific national concept (as deemed appropriate by the national legislator). Some examples of the linguistic changes involved are given in Chapter 4, in the section "A brief guide to Community legislation".

Eurospeak is also excusable when used to refer to genuinely "European" concepts that have no equivalent at national level; and they may be convenient because they avoid confusion. For example, "subsidiarity" (taking EU decisions and action at the lowest feasible regional, national or central level) is probably preferable to "devolution", which means the same, because in the UK, "devolution" is conventionally used to refer to relations with Scotland, Wales and Northern Ireland.

Example of a problem term:
"l'acquis communautaire"
The French expression *acquis* is very commonly used in the EU context, untranslated. It refers to the body of EU law (regulations, directives, decisions etc.) and the case law of the European Court of Justice, i.e. all EU legislation and rulings since the inception of the EU in the 1950s. It also has connotations of "all the things we have achieved, not without some difficulty". All that, in one six-letter word! Naturally EU insiders find it a very convenient term and use it frequently. We even use it ourselves occasionally in this book. But unfortunately it does not mean anything to outsiders. It can be particularly puzzling when used in speeches (*à qui? AKI? aquí?*). The writer of this section has been contacted by the Commission's Delegation in Washington, DC, with the plea to avoid the expression *acquis* in English texts for American readers, because they don't understand it. They are not alone: many European readers don't understand it either. Confusingly, it is spreading into derived expressions, such as "the Schengen *acquis*" (meaning the legislation and rulings adopted under the Schengen Convention).

Slogans and puns – mission impossible

As explained in Chapter 4, translators in the EU institutions do not spend all their time translating legislation. Many of our texts are "quasi-legal": they refer to EU legislation, or they use the same terminology (reports on the transposition of directives, for example, or Green or White Papers whose purpose is to consult the Member States on the desirability of introducing new legislation in the first place). But a sizeable chunk of our work is also intended for the general reader, and is written in an attempt to promote European integration and the work of the EU institutions. There are hundreds of booklets, databases and websites on EU projects and policies. Often they are produced by outside contractors, because it is generally assumed that the staff translators in the EU institutions are too busy (true) or too pedantic (untrue) to translate this type of material. The results are not always good. Many a promotional booklet has been pulped before it even reached the general public; many a staff translator has been called in to do a last-minute rescue job under difficult conditions; and plenty of inappropriate material still gets through. Non-translators (that is: people whose job is not translation, and whose skills and experience lie elsewhere) often underestimate the difficulty of translation, and they always underestimate the difficulty – or near impossibility – of translating promotional material into eleven or more languages.

Slogans and catchy titles are often genuinely untranslatable, because they are based on culture-specific connotations that don't exist in another culture, plays on words, or puns that don't work in another language. Puns pack several meanings into one word, and it is extremely unlikely that any other language will pack in the same set of meanings. It is often possible to re-invent slogans or puns in another language, but is this translation? Attention must also be paid to the cultural acceptability of puns and wordplay. In some cultures they are considered clever, in others they are regarded as superficial and undignified.

Example of a non-reproducible play on words:
le passage de l'écrit à l'écran (literally: the move from writing to screen).
This expression is used, in the context of libraries and text production, to refer to the changeover from paper-based to screen-based information sources.

In French, "**de l'écrit à l'écran**" is a nice catchphrase (although it does not stand up to close analysis: there is writing on the screen too). In some other Romance languages, it might just be possible to reproduce the play on words. Even in English, "**from screed to screen**" might work in those (very few) contexts where the word "screed" would not jar. In most contexts, however, it would be better to drop the alliteration and translate it, more prosaically, as "the changeover from paper to screen".

Example of an untranslatable pun:

"A gift of change"

Explanation: By donating your **change** (= coins) you can help to **change** (= transform) the lives of people in need.

This is a slogan used by Caritas International; it is printed on envelopes given to international travellers, inviting them to donate their surplus foreign-currency coins. On envelopes distributed in Germany, most of the text is in German, but the actual slogan is left in English. In EU texts, leaving slogans and titles in English is not an option. Apart from being incomprehensible to many readers, it would increase the strangeness of EU texts if words were left untranslated, and there would be accusations of cultural imperialism if those untranslated words were in English.

Even the most ordinary words – or perhaps one should say **especially** the most ordinary words – have different connotations in different countries.

Example: **bread**

As many authors have observed, the word *bread* conjures up something long, thin and crusty for the French; square, white and soggy for the British; black, round and heavy for the Germans. The concrete 'meaning' varies; but the symbolic status of bread, as the basic means of human sustenance, is the same for people throughout the Western world. So even if bread-as-an-object cannot always be translated – in recipes for example – bread-as-a-symbol will translate well enough.

Example: **green**

The word *green* is more problematic. Here the concrete meaning – having the colour green – is the same everywhere, perhaps thanks to chlorophyll. But the symbolic meaning varies. Imagine you have to translate a French publication with the title *L'Europe verte* (literal translation: *green Europe*). For the French and Spanish, the title *L'Europe verte* and *Europa verde* would be about agriculture. A German would assume that *Grünes Europa* is about conservation and the environment. What would a British or Irish reader make of *Green Europe*? Something to do with gardening or politics, maybe? The problem seems insoluble, especially as the word *green* has many other connotations too: *young, immature*, as in the Portuguese *vinho verde* (literal translation: *green wine*); in Spanish it can also mean *dirty* or *smutty* as in 'a dirty joke' (Spanish: *chiste verde*).

Example: **social**

This seemingly innocuous word has very different connotations in different countries (incidentally covering the entire political spectrum from the left-wing Socialists to the right-wing Christian Social parties found in several European countries). Until recently the English word *social* had quite frivolous associations (as in *social life* and *social animal*), and the worthy expressions *social affairs*, *social dialogue* and *social partners* appearing in EU texts were considered to be jargon or Eurospeak. Many native English speakers still prefer the traditional *both sides of industry*, with its sporting connotations of teams on opposing sides, to the continental *social partners*, which puts the two sides (employers and workers) into a perhaps unwilling partnership. Non-native speakers of English are often unaware that *both sides of industry* and *social partners* actually mean the same thing. Language changes: *social partners* may well catch on in Britain eventually. See the section below on **Interference by non-translators** for an illustration of how the Gallicism *democratic deficit* has caught on.

Crossing cultural barriers

All the EU institutions' activities involve intensive cooperation with outside contacts and therefore exchange of documents. The three directions of document flow are: incoming, outgoing, and internal. They present different sorts of cultural challenges.

Translating for in-house readers

In-house readers need translations of incoming texts that have been produced in the Member States and are submitted by national governments, ministries and members of the public. These are usually translated into one language for in-house information: either English or French. They are, accordingly, handled by English and French translators and are rarely encountered by translators working into other languages (except in the European Parliament, and the two Committees, the ESC and the COR, which still do a much larger proportion of translation into all languages). These texts may present problems, particularly if they are written in the translator's fifth or sixth foreign language, and s/he is unfamiliar with the national context. But help is readily available just down the corridor: we work in a multicultural environment, with colleagues from every Member State, all willing to help with linguistic and context problems – or even just deciphering a hand-written fax in their mother tongue.

Internal documents (in-house minutes, administrative information, etc.) are often left untranslated, or are translated only into French or English, and occasionally into German. When translating into a *lingua franca* such as English, it is advisable to bear in mind that most of one's readers will not be of English mother tongue, and will be puzzled by colloquialisms (however appropriate), topical allusions to British politics and TV programmes, and unusual words. Several of the most perplexing words begin with "a": akin, albeit, awry. Another frequently unrecognised word is "outwith" (for "outside"), as in "this matter is outwith our competence". These are all perfectly respectable words, and not even particularly rare, but they are best avoided, because they never fail to perplex. Many people just *think* they understand English, remember.

Translating for readers outside the EU institutions

Outgoing documents are texts written inside the institutions, usually in English or French, and translated into the other languages for readers in the Member States – and the target readers may range from top-notch specialists to schoolchildren. There is a rule that any important text forwarded to another institution (draft legislation, reports and White Papers) must be translated into all the official languages, as these texts will ultimately be made public – usually after some political haggling. Outgoing documents addressed to an individual or a single member state will be translated only into the language required.

In the EU institutions, most of the translators – with the exception of the French and English translators, for whom the situation is quite different, as already explained – spend most of their time translating outgoing documents. Much of their output will be published in the Official Journal, in glossy publications or on the Internet. Translators of outgoing documents face the most demanding readers, and the problem of "translating a different reality".

Example: **Charlemagne**
This different reality will include certain assumptions about the cultural and historical knowledge of readers. The historical figure Charlemagne is often mentioned in European propaganda, for reasons that will be clear from the following:
Charlemagne, Emperor Latin CAROLUS MAGNUS, meaning Charles the Great (...) King of the Franks 768 – 814, united by conquest nearly all Christian lands of western Europe (...); his reign was characterised by a brilliant court and by an imperial unity unrivalled for centuries before and after. (Source: Encyclopædia Britannica, Micropædia, Vol. 2:753)

Charlemagne is a familiar figure for French, Belgian and German readers; but Danes will not necessarily recognise him, and British readers will be more familiar with William the Conqueror and even the (Danish!) King Canute. Similarly, readers in eastern Europe may be unacquainted with Charlemagne and may feel excluded if he is mentioned.

Example: **maternity leave**
One achievement of the European Union has been to ensure that all workers in the EU are entitled to paid maternity leave for at least three months. But a speech or booklet full of self-congratulation on this achievement will not be well received in a country that already has a different reality (in Sweden it is normal to have one year's maternity leave).

In the above cases, conscientious translators should warn the author that the concept may not translate well, and try to suggest an alternative way of getting the same idea across.

Translating for ... who knows?

All the translation services have a system of workflow management, with an electronic worksheet on which the requester indicates:

* the document to be translated,
* languages required,
* deadline,
* reference documents,
* purpose of the translation (for comprehension, for information, for publication, for in-house readers or the general public etc.).

Unfortunately, the last two items – reference documents and purpose – do not always receive as much attention as translators would like, because requesters do not understand their importance. It is not uncommon for the "purpose" to be given as "committee meeting on 6 March". Of course, for many routine documents such as draft legislation, answers to parliamentary questions, annual reports and correspondence, the purpose and readership are clear and do not really need to be specified.

So although we understand the need to translate differently for different types of reader, and we ask to be informed about the purpose and target readers of our translations where it is not self-evident, we don't always get a clear answer. Sometimes this is because translation requesters don't understand why we need to know, or because they haven't thought about it yet. Sometimes it is quite simply because they are faced by a document they don't understand, so it is difficult to specify the purpose and target readership (all they can do at this stage is to specify "translation for comprehension").

The result of this is that we don't always know who the readers will be – or, indeed, if anyone will ever read our translations. Nor is it always fair to blame the requesters: they may not know either. It may depend how useful the document is – something that can only be judged after it has been translated into a language they can understand. It may be that a document – such as a national report on the impact of the euro in schools – is translated first as a working document for a committee. The committee may politely "take note" of the report and then consign it to the archives; or it may decide to publish it in glossy booklet form in every Member State.

Recently, printed paper has given way to Internet publishing, and this has helped in two ways. Firstly, it is cheaper than printing, and secondly, the text can still be improved: a provisional translation can be replaced by a more polished one. The Internet has helped in two other less obvious ways too:

- if the target readers are unspecified, translators can justifiably decide to write for the general reader rather than the specialist;
- we can check whether anyone "visits" the translation on the Internet, and we could invite feedback.

It would be inexcusable to waste translation resources on texts that no one reads. The EU institutions do not translate "for the archives", and always try to limit translation to the languages actually required. There are complaints when certain language versions are not available, and when some translations are in the form of summaries rather than the full text. There is no evidence that a significant percentage of our translations remains unread (although translators do sometimes quite wrongly suspect this). The only way to obtain this evidence would be by refusing to translate, and waiting for the reactions, or by carrying out the Internet checks suggested above. Suggestions that we should incorporate offers of "a free bottle of champagne for anyone who reads this far" are merely frivolous.

Quality of originals and the effect on translations

One factor that complicates life for translators working for the EU institutions is the poor quality and excessive length of some of the texts they are required to translate. Not only are these texts produced by authors with varying drafting skills, but in most cases the authors are unidentifiable: the texts are collectively produced with disparate input from various sources, in the process of consensus formation and political compromise. On top of this, word-processing allows texts to be tweaked and amended (not necessarily improved) up to the last possible minute, and the translations have to be amended to match. When the original texts are put together under such circumstances – and see the section on **"Deadlines"** below – the translations cannot possibly be as good as they would be if they were based on a final, polished text produced by a responsible, accessible author. It is demotivating for translators to have to translate texts that they know are excessively long and badly written. By way of reassurance, all one can say is that:

- it is an occupational hazard of working in the EU institutions;
- translation sometimes helps to demonstrate the weaknesses of a poor original;
- there are some things translators can do to rectify the situation.

Drafting by non-native speakers

Most of the texts written inside the EU institutions are produced in English or French by non-native speakers of those languages. In recent years, English has overtaken French as the main language of drafting in the EU institutions. In multinational drafting teams it is unreasonable to allow everyone to write their contribution in their mother tongue: it would take too long (because of translation), and would impose an additional burden on translation services that are already fully occupied. Nor, we are told, would it be acceptable for drafters to be nominated solely on grounds of nationality or even drafting skill. In fact many non-native speakers do a remarkably good job of drafting in English; and native speakers of English are not necessarily good writers. Everyone working in the EU institutions is subjected to a flood of Eurojargon, franglais and false friends, and it is difficult not to be swept along by the tide. It requires a conscious effort to remind oneself that

FR: *délai*   is   EN: deadline,   NOT "delay",
and
EN: delay   is   FR: *retard,*   NOT "*délai*"

This is especially difficult when so many papers have been published, written by non-native (or gone-native?) speakers, referring to "payment delays" when they really meant "payment periods". Naturally, translators who dare to complain about these mistakes are labelled hairsplitters and pedants (FR: *pédants pinailleurs*), but it is a badge we should wear with pride.

There are inevitably problems of interpretation when translating texts written by non-native speakers. To continue with the above example: the French translator has to decide whether the English word "delay" is being used correctly by the author, and should be translated by the French "*retard*", or if it is being wrongly used and should be translated by "*délai*". The general context will provide some clues, as will the quality of the rest of the text and the name of the author (if it is known). At the same time, the French translator's colleagues who are translating the same text into the other nine official languages will be having to take the same decisions and do the same detective work – and, one hopes, arriving at the same conclusions, although there is no guarantee that they will. (For important texts, collation meetings can be arranged to iron out difficulties.) Much expensive translator time is spent dealing with problems of this kind. Rushed drafting and poor originals certainly augment the cost of translation in the EU institutions.

Collective drafting

Everyone knows that a camel is a horse invented by a committee. EU documents are invented by many committees; then passed to other EU institutions for rewriting by *their* committees; and finally haggled over by politicians – often late at night or early in the morning – with planes to catch, a point to be made beforehand, and no time to read the whole thing carefully.

Translations have to be produced at most stages in the life of these documents, following their tortuous progress so that they can be understood and
re-hashed by the Members of the European Parliament (who are not, and should
not be, elected for their foreign language skills) and the national ministers meeting
in the Council.

This is a pessimistic picture, and applies only to political and legal material.
Many other texts, such as reports, letters and public information, have a simpler
and more straightforward gestation. But collective drafting is a common practice, as in all international organisations and civil services. It is assumed that a
patchwork of input and a succession of amendments will make for a better and
more balanced text; and that including them all will ensure that the end result is
acceptable to all parties. In fact this practice, also called "consensus building",
makes for excessively long documents of uneven style, in which the original
argument has been distorted or submerged by provisos. Worst of all, there is no
longer a single author willing to put his or her name to the end result; the camel
has become the collective responsibility of a department or an institution.

On the optimistic side, it is only fair to point out that collective drafting *can*
make for better texts: two (or twenty) heads *can* be better than one. Take the
typical political speech prepared for a Commissioner: it starts its life with the
speechwriter, who draws on factual input from technical specialists; then the
Commissioner's political advisers will check and amend the contents; it may
then be translated or edited by a native speaker; and finally the Commissioner
will make his or her own amendments either before or during delivery. This is a
perfectly efficient way of working, as long as there is no denial of responsibility
(in this case, the Commissioner accepts it). And it would be hypocritical to
criticise collective drafting in a book that is being written by three authors – a
Dane, a Spaniard, and a Briton (and edited by an Australian – cripes!) – in the
hope that this will produce a more balanced and interesting result.

New drafting guidelines for legislation, clear writing campaigns

All the EU institutions are aware of the difficulties mentioned above, and provide training for their officials in English and French drafting. Even Commission
Presidents have found time to comment on the problem: President Delors urged
Commission staff to "write with a lighter pen" and President Santer's dictum
that we should do "less, but better" was intended to apply to document production as well as other activities. President Prodi is so interested in clarity that he
overhauled the entire Press and Communications Service soon after he was
appointed. Successive Secretaries-General (the Secretary-General is the most
senior civil servant in the Commission) have tried, so far in vain, to impose
limits on the length of Commission documents (20 pages is often mentioned).
Some Members of the European Parliament have also been very active in pro-

moting clarity and accessibility. Several European countries have plain language movements pushing for clearer communication in the interests of democracy, and Eurospeak is increasingly coming under fire.

Two recent initiatives, one serious and one more light-hearted, are the Interinstitutional Agreement on the Quality of Legal Drafting, and the Fight the FOG campaign.

Interinstitutional Agreement on the quality of legal drafting

The Amsterdam Treaty, signed in October 1997, included a Declaration (No 39) on the quality of drafting of Community legislation, saying:

"The Conference notes that the quality of the drafting of Community legislation is crucial if it is to be properly implemented by the competent national authorities and better understood by the public and business circles.

(...)

"Therefore, the Conference declares that the European Parliament, the Council and the Commission ought to:

– establish by common accord guidelines for improving the quality of the drafting of Community legislation and follow those guidelines when considering proposals for Community legislation or draft legislation, taking the internal organisational measures they deem necessary to ensure that these guidelines are properly applied; (...)". (Official Journal No C 340, 10.11.1997:139)

The common guidelines were duly produced in December 1998 by the legal services of the three main institutions (Council, Parliament and Commission) in the form of an Interinstitutional Agreement on common guidelines for the quality of drafting of Community legislation. It was published in Official Journal No C 73, dated 17.3.1999:1.

It sets out many excellent general principles:

"Community legislative acts shall be drafted clearly, simply and precisely." (...)

"Overly long articles and sentences, unnecessarily convoluted wording and excessive use of abbreviations should be avoided." (...)

"... concepts or terminology specific to any one national legal system are to be used with care."

However, it does not recommend any sweeping changes: it re-states the existing rules for legislative drafting, introduces some innovations in paragraph numbering, and concludes with a list of implementing measures, recommending training in legal drafting, the creation of dedicated drafting units, and "cooperation with the Member States with a view to improving understanding of the particular considerations to be taken into account when drafting texts."

The word "translation" does not appear anywhere in the Interinstitutional Agreement.

Fight the FOG campaign

Fight the FOG is a grass-roots campaign for clear writing in the European Commission. It was started in 1998 by Commission translators who were worried that the European Union's message was not getting across to the general public because it was obscured by "FOG". This is a metaphor for the grey pall that descends on Commission documents, causing delays and irritation, making it difficult to find one's way. FOG is also an acronym for "farrago of Gallicisms", "frequency of gobbledygook", "full of garbage" etc.

The campaign organisers decided to mount a campaign to raise awareness of the difference between "real English" and what was being written in Commission documents. They wanted to provide concrete advice on how to write clearly and succinctly, and to attack on several fronts, preferably in an amusing way, without causing too much offence. The campaign included:

- lectures by writers, politicians and clear language experts;
- a free booklet on "How to Write Clearly", 10 000 copies distributed;
- courses on clear writing for Commission staff;
- a website (http://europa.eu.int/comm/translation/en/ftfog) with links to the lectures, reports, the booklet, a list of frequently misused words and a collection of humour.

The results of any campaign are difficult to measure (how much worse would things have been if it hadn't taken place?) but FOG-fighting activities are continuing and diversifying, highlighting the importance of writing clearly and demonstrating how to do it.

One element of the campaign is an occasional column called the "Fog-Fighting Corner" in the Commission's staff magazine *Commission en Direct*. This presents a piece of typical Euro-fog and invites readers to produce a clearer version. Here is an example:

FOGGY TEXT:
The General Affairs Council's central responsibility for general horizontal issues, including overall policy co-ordination, means it will have to manage an increasingly external and internal agenda, dealing with major multidisciplinary and interpillar dossiers. Effectively handling all aspects of its work by better agenda management and suitable Member State representation is essential if the General Affairs Council is to continue to play its role in assuring overall co-ordination and policy consistency and in preparing European Council meetings.

(Source: Communiqué outlining the results of the Helsinki European Council, quoted in a letter to *The Times* on 22 December 1999 by Lord Bruce of Donington, a member of the British House of Lords. He complained that it was incomprehensible.)

One of the best versions submitted by readers was this:

CLEAR TEXT:
The General Affairs Council coordinates issues that cut across different policy areas. So it is going to have to tackle business not only from inside the EU, but increasingly from outside. To keep policy consistent and prepare European Council meetings, it will have to manage its agenda better, and make sure Member States send the right people to discussions.

Editing of originals

Translators are expected to translate originals in full, however wordy and badly phrased. But in view of the difficulties mentioned above – drafting by non-native speakers, patchwork drafting, etc. – some of the EU institutions' translation services now offer editing or "rewriting" as a standard service for authors. The options range from systematic editing of English originals before translation (as at the Court of Auditors and the European Central Bank) to "linguistic revision" carried out when, and only when, it has been specifically requested by the client (as at the Commission).

Editing by translators is a relatively new activity, and many clients are unaware that it is available. One of the effects of the Fight the FOG campaign at the Commission has been to draw clients' attention to the existence of this service. Nevertheless, it comes up against a number of problems:

- the need for a clearer definition of "editing": the service can range from surface correction of errors and "non-native" turns of phrase to radical rewriting and shortening;
- the need to develop translators' editing skills, by experience and training;
- the fact that editing must be done before translation is started, and can curtail the time available for translation;
- the reluctance of authors to accept this type of correction, because they do not trust translators to understand the nuances of their texts (in which case, one wonders, how are we supposed to translate them?).

A very rare practice, and one that also depends on trust and mutual respect, is the inclusion of translators in drafting teams. This can help to obviate problems of quality and translatability. Editing is always more successful when the authors are there to explain unclear passages and/or sanction alternative wording.

Interference

This section outlines a number of occupational hazards that have one thing in common: they can all be described as forms of interference.

Interference between languages

Everyone working in a multilingual environment risks some erosion of their ability to speak and write their mother tongue. This is because of interference from other languages: the invasion of foreign vocabulary and syntax; exposure to the frequent misuse of their mother tongue; the effects of fatigue and compromise; and the desire not to appear pedantic. Translators are no exception to this general rule. But one hopes that translators can learn to resist this danger and develop conscious strategies to maintain their mother-tongue skills by:

- reading their national press – not just for information, but as linguists, actively analysing the way their own language is used;
- maintaining links with their home country – not just for the obvious human reasons, but again, in order to observe how their country's language and national attitudes are changing.

One also hopes that they will be more discerning than the administrative and political staff in the EU institutions, who are not professional linguists.

The problems of drafting by non-native speakers have already been discussed in the section above on "Quality of originals". It is perhaps useful at this point to list some of the most prevalent "false friends" – cases where there is a misleading resemblance between a French word and an English one, leading to interference between the two languages.

French	**Incorrect English**	**Correct English**
actuel	actual	current, topical
adéquat	adequate	suitable
assister à	assist at	attend, participate
capacité	capacity	ability, capability
compléter	complete	supplement
contrôler	control	supervise, check
disposer de	dispose of	have, keep
éventuel	eventual	any
important	important	large
opportunité	opportunity	advisability
prévu	foreseen	provided for

These are some of the words most commonly misused in the EU institutions (extract from the Fight the FOG booklet, "How to Write Clearly"); needless to say, the correct English term suggested is not always correct, but it is usually preferable to the incorrect one.

Another kind of interference between languages is the "spill-over" of English and French terms into the other official languages. Politicians, journalists and other non-translators (see the section below on "Interference by non-translators") often select the obvious translations of French and English concepts discussed at meetings in the EU institutions, and will continue to use them in speeches and articles in their home country, instead of using the correct terms which feature in the Treaties and are faithfully reproduced by translators.

Examples: **Interference between English/French terms and Danish**
1. The term "implementation" is correctly rendered as *gennemførelse* in the Danish version of the EC Treaty and in other texts produced by Danish translators. Politicians and journalists tend to use the term *implementering* and the derived verb *implementere*.
2. Similarly, the term "notification" is correctly rendered as *meddelelse* in the EC Treaty and in other official texts, but Danish politicians and journalists normally say *notifikation* when speaking or writing in (pseudo-)Danish.

Similar temptations exist in all languages.

Interference between registers

Interference between registers is a more sensitive matter, and one that does not appear to be generally recognised. It comes about when terms and stylistic features that would be appropriate in a specialised context (a legal document, for example) are allowed to spill over into a more general context, where they will not be understandable – or may even be alienating – for the target reader. Conversely, if colloquial or journalistic expressions are used in a specialised document, they may irritate the readers or make the author or translator seem less credible.

Example: **natural or legal persons**
The following sentence is taken from an information leaflet (written in English by a non-native speaker) for people interested in bidding for service contracts with the EU institutions:
"Service providers may be either **natural or legal persons**, and assignments can be awarded irrespective of the place of residence of the service provider in the EU."

This is correct legalese, but it is not informative. It is used in an information leaflet, not an actual contract. In order to inform, it should say:

"Contracts may be awarded to **individuals or companies** located anywhere in the EU."

Although English-speaking lawyers would no doubt understand what is meant by a "natural or legal person", the majority of English readers won't understand. In fact they would probably be quite surprised to learn that they are "natural persons" (individuals) as opposed to "legal persons" (companies).

Example: **Official names of countries (the United Kingdom, the Netherlands**, etc.)

For political reasons, the official name of every Member State must be learned by EU officials at an early stage and used unfailingly in all texts. Translators soon learn to write "the Netherlands" instead of "Holland", and "the United Kingdom" instead of "Britain" or "England". The trouble is that these official names are not meaningful to all sectors of the public. The register-conscious translator should be aware that when translating an information booklet for schoolchildren, for example, it will be more effective to use the common names – Holland, Britain, etc. – than the official ones (possibly adding a translator's note somewhere in the small print, to justify the choice).

It is virtually impossible to select the right register if, as sometimes happens, we do not know who the target readers are.

Interference by non-translators

Translation is not a high-prestige profession, and even though it is essential to the functioning of the EU institutions, translators are no more highly regarded here than in the outside world. Perhaps less so, because our non-translator colleagues are all polyglots too, and they see translation as something they could do for themselves "if they had the time". Sometimes they do try their hand at it, producing their own translations or "improving" ours (or they ask their secretaries or trainees to do so instead). And the result is the dreaded "grey translation" – somewhere between the official snow-white product and unofficial black translation.

No translator objects to real improvements and feedback. If there is a mistake in a translation, we are only too happy for the requester to let us know, so we can put it right. But "grey translation" is not the same thing. If requesters or their secretaries change our translations without informing us, they may delete terminology that has been established after hours of research and consultation with national experts, or distort the register of the text by introducing bureaucratic jargon that is used in-house but means nothing outside.

As things stand at present, translators in some EU institutions have no control over the versions of their translations that are published. In the European Parliament, Council and Court of Justice, the translation services do have final responsibility for translations. In the Commission, however, the texts belong not to the translation service but to the author departments responsible for them. Two examples will serve to illustrate the problem; in both cases they are the titles of publications, and thus particularly obvious and painful for translators (and, of course, for readers):

Examples of interference by non-translators: **grey translation of titles**

Example 1 dates from 1975. A secretary in the Commission's radiation protection directorate had sent the contents of the "*Bulletin signalétique de la radioprotection*" for translation, but had forgotten to send the title page, so she produced her own translation:
  "**Radioprotection's Signalled Bulletin**". (A better English title would have been "Abstracts on Radiation Protection".)

Example 2 is more recent. The Commission's "*Fil d'Ariane*" on consumer protection was sent for translation in 1999 and the title was translated as "Consumer's Guide" in English and as "Ein praktischer Ratgeber" in German. But when the booklet was published in 2000, the English title had become the nonsensical "**A Labyrinthian Thread**" and the German "**Der Faden der Ariadne**". The titles suggested by the translators were obviously too prosaic!
  (The French title "*Fil d'Ariane*" does indeed mean "Ariadne's thread" and "der Faden der Ariadne". It is an expression very commonly used in French (almost a cliché) to refer to any guide through any kind of administrative or technical maze. But it does not have the same meaning for English-speaking and German-speaking readers, perhaps because they are less familiar with Greek mythology. It harks back to the tale of Theseus's visit to the Minotaur's labyrinth; a thread provided by his girlfriend Ariadne helped him to find his way out of the labyrinth once he had killed the Minotaur.)

Another form of interference by non-translators is their insistence on certain expressions "because that is what we call it in our committee and we all know what it means". The terminology concocted in committee meetings – often conducted in a *lingua franca* such as English or French, because interpretation has to be reserved for high-level committees – is naturally full of false friends and would yield rich pickings for research on interference between languages.

Example: "**the democratic deficit**"
The expression "the democratic deficit" is a straight translation from the French

"*le déficit démocratique*". It was first used in a European Parliament committee, which then insisted that the Parliament translators use the same expression
in their translations. When the English translators pointed out that it meant nothing in English, and proposed "**the democracy gap**" instead, they were given
short shrift. The committee had always talked about the democratic deficit, and
so it had to remain. With the result that until recently it was always mentioned
in inverted commas in the British press – another odd Eurocratic coinage.

It now seems to have entered the English language, though: in a debate in
the UK Parliament in February 2000, an MP spoke about "the democratic deficit" in Northern Ireland.

(Extract from on-line Hansard (UK House of Commons debates) for 8 February 2000, Column 139:

> Mr. MacKay: " ... This is an extremely sad day for the people of North-
> ern Ireland. They, naturally, yearn for a lasting peace, and they have hoped
> and prayed for decommissioning. They have been dreadfully let down.
> Over the past few weeks, they have enjoyed having their own Executive
> and elected Assembly. The **democratic deficit** that I consider to have
> been so damaging to the body politic in Northern Ireland had been
> eradicated, and we saw Northern Ireland's elected politicians taking
> responsibility for much that happened in the Province. That was healthy,
> right and proper ... ")

Deadlines

Of all the problems encountered by translators working for the EU institutions,
public enemy number one is the unreasonable deadlines by which we have to
provide translations. Deadlines dominate all our work. Our requesters' maxim
is: an imperfect translation delivered on time is much better than a perfect one
delivered too late. The greatest efforts are made to secure reasonable deadlines,
so that we can deliver reasonable quality. We encourage requesters to plan ahead
and to set priorities. We remind them that they should finish writing their report
by date X if they want it to be translated by the ministers' meeting on date Y.
But ultimately, the EU institutions (especially the Council, Parliament and Commission) are political bodies subject to unpredictable pressures and events, and
translation just has to keep up. It is easy to blame bad planning – but no one
could have planned ahead for Kosovo or the BSE crisis (BSE = bovine
spongiform encephalopathy or "mad cow disease".)

Word processing has made it possible to amend texts up to the last minute,
and requesters make ample use of this facility. It is not unusual for a text to go
through six or seven successive versions (with accompanying translations) before reaching its final form. Eighteen versions is the record so far. It would be

logical (and more economical) to postpone translation until the original text has been finalised. But in reality, translations may be needed at the preliminary stages to permit discussion of the text; every version is optimistically assumed to be the final one; and there is very little time for translation after the text has been finalised. For example, in January 2000 the Commission adopted a White Paper (50 pages long) setting up a European Food Authority. It was written in English; the final amendments came in at 8.30 in the morning of the day when the Commission was meeting to adopt it. The French and German translations had to be completed for the press conference at 12.00 the same day.

Exercises for students

5.   Problems

5.1   Research
5.1.1. Find five slogans (advertising or political) in your first foreign language – in the press or on the Internet. Proceed to Exercise 5.3.1 below.

5.1.2 Find some material on Europa or in printed EU publicity that is written in an unattractive style. Suggest improvements.

5.2   Terminology
5.2.1 Produce a three-language glossary of the following terms: "governance", "civil society", "subsidiarity", with a definition of each in your mother tongue. (Hint: "Subsidiarity" is mentioned in Article 5 of the EC Treaty).

5.2.2 The various connotations of the word "green" in different languages are discussed in this chapter. Pick another colour and (with the help of a dictionary) produce a list of its connotations in two or more languages.

5.3   Translation
5.3.1 Translate the five slogans you found in 5.1.1 into your mother tongue, in such a way that they work as slogans. Proceed to Exercise 5.4.1 or 5.5.1

5.3.2 In an encyclopædia in your first foreign language, find a short (150 word) text about Charlemagne. Translate it into your mother tongue in a way that would be comprehensible for a 10-year-old child (e.g. for a school textbook).

5.4   Tools
5.4.1 Obtain a raw machine translation of your five slogans (Exercises 5.1.1 and 5.3.1) or of the Charlemagne extract (Exercise 5.3.2). Use a "Compare documents" tool (as available in Word / Tools / Track changes) to compare the machine translation with your own translation.

5.4.2 Take a short (150 word) extract from the Interinstitutional Agreement on the Quality of Legal Drafting – available on Europa, OJ reference given in Chapter 5 – and run it though a standard style checker or grammar checker. Look at the "improvements" suggested by the software and say how many of them are realistic.

5.5   Debate

5.5.1 If you decide that one or more of the five slogans selected in Exercise 5.1.1 and translated in Exercise 5.3.1 is untranslatable, discuss how you would explain this to a translation requester or client, assuming they do not understand the target language.

5.5.2 "Eurospeak is permissible between consenting adults". Discuss.

6. What the job involves

Day-to-day

This section does not attempt to give an exhaustive account of each translation service's organisational structure. That would be pointless: all organisations are subject to change. Instead we mention and explain some general features that are common to all the EU translation services, and some differences. We try to highlight points that might be surprising to outsiders and newcomers starting work in the services.

Organisation of work

At present all EU institutions require translators to translate into their mother tongue, and this is reflected in the standard organisational structure. Almost without exception, translators work in teams (called "units" or "divisions") made up of translators working into the same target language, and managed by a boss ("head of unit" or "head of division") who has spent most of his or her career working as a translator into that language. This single-language environment often comes as a surprise to newcomers who had been looking forward to working in a multinational and multilingual team. It is of course possible – and indeed necessary – to establish contacts with translators working into other languages, but one's immediate colleagues will be of the same mother tongue and often of the same nationality too. Obviously the language-to-nationality match is not one-to-one:

Target language	Usual nationality mix in translation team
Danish	Danish
German	German + Austrian + Belgian + Luxembourgish
English	British + Irish
Greek	Greek
Spanish	Spanish
French	French + Belgian + Luxembourgish
Italian	Italian
Dutch	Dutch + Belgian
Portuguese	Portuguese
Finnish	Finnish
Swedish	Swedish + Finnish

The usual reasons advanced for these single-language teams are:
*   easier administration and supervision of translation work;

- need for assistance from more experienced colleagues;
- easier access to library and documentation facilities in the appropriate language;
- maintenance of mother tongue by immersion in it. This is important. Almost all translators in Brussels and Luxembourg are outside their mother-tongue environment, and many of them speak another language at home, e.g. if married to someone of another nationality.

So most of the EU institutions' translation services have eleven translation divisions, one for each language. The exceptions to this rule are the small services (Court of Auditors, European Investment Bank, Translation Centre) and the largest one (European Commission). The small services, which may have only three or four translators per language, have a single translation division covering all languages. The Commission's translation service, being much larger, is divided into several departments or "thematic groups", each serving a certain subset of Commission Directorates-General and specialising in their subject areas (such as competition, agriculture or technology). Each department has eleven language units; at present there are six departments: four in Brussels and two in Luxembourg.

The "hierarchy" within the translation teams is simple and fairly flat: a typical team in the Commission has about 15 translators, graded differently to reflect their length of service, but all doing essentially the same job (translation and revision), 3 or 4 secretaries doing clerical and administrative work, and one head of unit. The European Parliament has divisions with about 40 translators, a pool of about 15 secretaries, one head of division and one deputy head of division. The translation teams concentrate on producing translations. Each unit or division will have a mix of expertise: enough translators to translate out of all the official languages, or at least the main languages requested, and enough revision capacity to provide quality control of its own production (time permitting). The translation teams are not responsible for general administrative activities such as training or recruitment, and there are separate departments for the necessary support staff such as librarians, terminologists and computer technicians.

To our surprise, outsiders imagine it must be very complicated to translate out of 11 languages and into 11 languages. But in fact the basic principle is very simple. The central role in the organisation of translation work is played by the "Planning" offices. They receive translation requests and channel them to the appropriate units, depending on the target languages requested.

The Planning offices are the main point of contact with the requesting services. They play an important role in explaining procedures, filtering out superfluous translation requests (e.g. texts which have already been translated), discouraging the submission of over-long texts (perhaps arranging to translate just the executive summary), and above all, negotiating translation deadlines. Requesters often leave too little time for translation and have to be "educated" into an understanding that translation cannot be provided instantly.

Example: English original to be translated into all official languages:

			→ Danish unit	**Danish translation**
			→ German unit	**German translation**
			English unit	
English text for translation into all official languages	→	**PLANNING OFFICE**	→ Greek unit	**Greek translation**
			→ Spanish unit	**Spanish translation**
			→ French unit	**French translation**
			→ Italian unit	**Italian translation**
			→ Dutch unit	**Dutch translation**
			→ Portuguese unit	**Portuguese translation**
			→ Finnish unit	**Finnish translation**
			→ Swedish unit	**Swedish translation**

Example: Greek original to be translated into English, French and German:

			Danish unit	
			→ German unit	**German translation**
			→ English unit	**English translation**
Greek text for translation into English, French and German	→	**PLANNING OFFICE**	Greek unit	
			Spanish unit	
			→ French unit	**French translation**
			Italian unit	
			Dutch unit	
			Portuguese unit	
			Finnish unit	
			Swedish unit	

The staff of the Planning offices – usually clerical staff rather than linguists – also have to check page counts, compare different versions of documents to identify amendments, and check document formats. All this can be done electronically. They also have more mundane but equally important tasks which cannot be done electronically, such as finding out the purpose of the translation, if it has not been made clear, and even identifying the source language of a text. Requesters sometimes confuse Spanish and Portuguese, or Swedish and Danish.

In-house or freelance?

There are some institutions, including the Council, that do not use freelance translation. In those that do, the procedure is as follows. Once a job has been accepted by the Planning office and directed to the appropriate translation units, it will be vetted by the head of unit to check its suitability for freelance translation. If it is not confidential, politically sensitive or hyper-urgent, if translating it does not call for too much inside information, if a reliable freelance translator is available and willing to accept the text – a lot of "ifs" – the head of unit may decide to send it to freelance. He or she will also take account of the expected in-house workload and the need to maintain in-house productivity.

The Translation Centre in Luxembourg has an approach to freelance translation which differs somewhat from that of the older translation services. From the outset, the Centre has regarded its external service providers as an essential part of its workforce rather than as emergency assistance, in the belief that this ensures better relations and a better level of service from its freelance contractors. Whilst in some cases the decision to outsource is based on the simple fact that the language combination and/or the area of specialisation concerned cannot be handled in-house, certain types of document are always outsourced, in particular regular publications (newsletters, annual reports, etc.) produced by the Centre's clients. This ensures, within the limits of the rules governing the management of public contracts, a regular supply of work for freelancers and a higher level of quality. As a rule of thumb, all projected documents (i.e. those notified to the Centre by its clients at the beginning of the year) and all documents more than ten pages long are outsourced, so that in-house translators can be kept available for dealing with urgent work and checking and, if necessary, revising outsourced translations.

Work distribution
Texts that are kept in-house are then passed on to the translators by the head of unit or by a specially designated coordinator. Some units have a self-service system allowing translators to choose their own work; others have a strict top-down system of distribution by the head of unit. The majority work with a hybrid arrangement under which some texts – extremely urgent jobs, for example – are given directly to translators and others are put into a "To be translated" tray from which translators can take their pick.

Revision policy
Revision is organised in a similarly flexible way – sometimes given directly to a certain reviser, sometimes arranged by self-service from a "To be revised" tray, and sometimes not done at all: if time is short, if the translator is an old hand, or if the declared purpose of translation does not merit full revision (e.g. translation for information only). There are some units, however, in which every single translation is revised or checked by another translator before it goes out. Even some very busy teams manage to have every translation looked at by two pairs of eyes. The quality gains seem to offset the slight delays; and getting junior

translators to read through translations by more experienced staff is a useful form of training. There is no "reviser caste" in the EU institutions; senior staff are expected to translate as well as revise. Junior staff may be encouraged to revise or check translations produced by their more experienced colleagues, both for training and because they bring a fresh eye: they have not yet been corrupted by Eurospeak, so they can often improve translations intended for the general public. See the section below, "In-house training" for some tips on coping with revision.

Interaction with clients

Another surprise awaiting idealistic newcomers to the EU translation services is this: the scarcity of contact with our "clients". In the proper sense, our clients should be our readers – the end users in the Member States. But in practice our clients are the "requesters": people working in the administrative departments of the institutions who need translations in order to do their job. Occasionally, they need translations because they cannot understand the language of the original (for example, a report written in Greek explaining how regional fund grants have been spent in the past six months). In the majority of cases, however, they understand the original perfectly, because they wrote it, or they are responsible for the committee that wrote it. They need translation in order to fulfil the formal requirement that documents be published or submitted for approval in several languages. In such circumstances, many of our clients view translation as a necessary evil that just delays the publication or adoption of their carefully-crafted text. In organisations where everyone knows several languages (no monoglots are recruited by the EU institutions, even at the lowest grades), there is no particular kudos attached to being a linguist

Translators masochistically revel in the insults thrown at them. When we complain about incomprehensible originals, we often get the plaintive reply: "Why can't you just translate it?" Or worse: "You don't have to understand it – just translate it!" Not all requesters are demons – some do appreciate the service we provide and even send messages of gratitude when their documents are delivered on time. But deadlines are paramount, and quality is taken for granted.

Inevitably, when day-to-day dealings with clients are in the hands of our Planning offices (see above), there is little direct contact with translators. If a document has to be produced in all the eleven official languages, there will be ten different translators working on it at the same time. If all ten were to phone the requester to ask the same questions about the text, he or she would be bound to get a little impatient. Therefore we try to arrange things so that a permanent or specially designated coordinator or a terminologist asks the questions on behalf of all the translators and passes on the answers.

Some institutions organise collation meetings at which all the translators get together to discuss a job, ideally in the presence of the author or the requester. This type of contact is extremely useful for all concerned, but it is still the exception rather than rule, because of the time constraints involved. The smaller institutions have greater scope for this type of arrangement and the Court of Auditors has set an excellent example here, based on an idea that came originally from the European Parliament.

Translation tools and aids used in the EU institutions

For some reason, many newcomers to the EU institutions' translation services expect us to be under-equipped with computer aids. The truth is that we have never in fact worked with quill pens. Ever since PCs have been cheap, every translator has had one, networked and linked to various servers and the Internet. Nor is there any resistance to using them.

Inputting translations

Even translators who prefer to dictate their first draft can and do use PCs for research, communication and to incorporate corrections to the final version of their translation. Translators are free to choose the working method that suits them best: there is no coercion to dictate or type one's texts. All translation units have secretaries willing to do audiotyping, and we are experimenting with speech recognition software for direct input. The majority of translators do, however, prefer to input their own texts. The vast majority of original texts are now available in electronic form and a popular (but not universal) method of inputting, for translators or audiotypists, is overtyping the original text. This makes it easier to conserve formatting and layout (which may be fairly complicated, and a pain to reproduce).

In addition to straight word-processing software, translators in some but not all institutions have access to other "ongoing translations" of the same text and to shared files with translators' and terminologists' comments on problems and solutions for each document. Many documents are simultaneously being translated into ten languages: it makes sense for all the translators to be able to consult each other's efforts so far, and to share information gleaned from the author, translation requester or terminologist.

Research

The Internet (together with in-house Intranets) is now the main research tool for translators in most institutions. Not only are search engines much used, but the Internet also increasingly serves as a gateway to the terminology databases created by EU institutions in pre-Internet days (Eurodicautom, TIS, EUTERPE). As well as improving access to these traditional databases and opening up access to resources not previously available (such as the shared corpus of international organisations' terminology compiled under the auspices of JIAMCATT – the Joint Inter-Agency Meeting on Computer-Aided Translation and Terminology), Internet technologies have made it possible to develop terminology "metasearch" facilities which rationalise access to information (one question – many bases searched) and to plan for terminology data entry directly over the Web, more or less a *sine qua non* for the projected interinstitutional termbase. More mundanely, we also have many CD-ROM dictionaries with shared electronic access and, of course, libraries containing paper versions of dictionaries and glossaries.

Full-text databases and document collections

One of the most useful resources in any translation service has always been the shared archive of completed translations. Now that it is no longer in paper files, but in electronic form, with indexing and parallel searching of different language versions, it can be shared, maintained and searched much more rapidly and efficiently.

The essential full-text databases, available on-line for rapid searching in all official languages, are CELEX (electronic collection of all EU legislation and case law) and EUR-Lex (Treaties, recent Official Journals, legislation in force, consolidated texts, preparatory acts and recent case law). Both of these are available on the Internet and can be used by freelance translators too (though access to CELEX is not free of charge for the general public). In addition we have some similar applications that have to be restricted to in-house users because they contain "official documents in progress", such as SG-Vista, a repository of ongoing official documents in the Commission.

Translation memories

A logical extension of electronic archives is the "translation memory" which contains matched sentences from past translations, in source and target languages. If a given sentence has been translated before and stored in the translation memory, it can be retrieved and injected into a new translation. This saves time and improves consistency. Most of the EU institutions are now investing in translation memory software and planning to share each other's memories. The European Commission has used software of this type for several years. With repetitive documents (annual or monthly reports, for example), up to 40% (even more in particularly favourable cases) of the "new" text can be recreated from past versions and offered to translators either interactively as they type in their word-processing software or in the form of a "preprocessed" version of the original. In either case, text will typically be shown in different colours depending on whether it is a proposed translation for an exactly matching sentence, a translation for a similar sentence ("fuzzy" match) or a sentence for which no match has been found.

This facility is not restricted to in-house translators: freelances may also find they are offered texts including up to 40% pre-processing – with a reduction in their fee. Naturally, even the pre-processed segments have to be checked and may need to be adapted (if the new text is written for a different audience, for example). But for translators new to the institutions, or tackling a new subject field, this is a very powerful tool.

Electronic documentation through hyperlinks
Some applications are being developed which provide hyperlinks to documentation. For example, the European Court of Justice has developed a tool in-house for this purpose called GTi (Generic Text interface). For reasons of legal consistency, Court translators must cite the same source documents as authors, but in the appropriate language version. With GTi, the full electronic documentation used by the author is made available to the translators through hyperlinks in the text that can be "switched" to whichever language version is required.

Machine translation
The EU institutions, especially the Commission, lead the field in machine translation development and use. Since 1976, Systran has been about to put EU translators out of work. Yet we are still there ... and so is Systran. Now called EC-Systran, a proprietary version which is superior to the Internet version, it works in the following language pairs:

Source	> Target languages:
English	> French, German, Dutch, Spanish, Portuguese, Italian, Greek (test)
French	> English, German, Dutch, Spanish, Portuguese, Italian
German	> English and French
Spanish	> English and French
Greek (test)	> French

Systran is used in the following ways in the EU institutions:

Raw translations: Anyone, in any department, can obtain raw translations instantly, on-line, without formalities. Most requesters see the limitations of raw machine translation and understand that it cannot be used without post-editing, except perhaps for information scanning. Some requesters use it as a drafting aid – they may prefer to write a letter or manual in French, if that is their stronger language, and then use Systran to help them produce an English version.

Rapid post-editing: As an adjunct to raw translation, requesters have the option of obtaining a rapidly post-edited version within a few days. This service is offered by the Commission's Translation Service and normally provided by selected freelance translators who have put in a bid for this type of work (which is less well paid than full translation). The service is fairly popular, but it is not suitable for publications or legal texts, and much of our work now comes into those categories.

As an aid to full-quality translation: All translators can obtain raw Systran translations in the above language pairs and use them as a basis for a human-quality translation. But surprisingly few choose to do so, even *in extremis*. It is generally felt that Systran works reasonably well between related languages (especially Romance languages with similar syntactic structures), and this is reflected in the translators' take-up of the product. French into Spanish is the most popular language pair. French into Italian also works well, but is less used. English into Spanish is popular too: the Spanish translators are generally more enthusiastic about machine translation and have invested a great deal of time and effort in developing the dictionaries. But any language pair involving German as source or target seems to be unpopular; and the English and French translators are less enamoured of Systran, despite the quarter-century of development that has gone into English and French as source and target languages.

In-house training

Translation is the sort of profession where you never stop learning. People who want to feel that they "know it all" at the age of 25 had better not consider becoming translators. Almost every text you translate brings new knowledge – a deeper understanding of the source language, stretching your active knowledge of the target language, learning unfamiliar terminology, and adding to your world knowledge. Pension schemes in China? Birdstrike statistics? Digital TV? Ice-cream manufacture? Those were the topics a few of our colleagues were immersing themselves in last week, as they translated texts on those subjects. For freelance and staff translators alike, it is this opportunity to learn that makes our job so interesting. Most of this new knowledge is gained not by formal training but by individual research, such as library searches, contacts with authors and in-house specialists, e-mails to experts in our home countries and most recently, searches on the Internet.

The institutions also offer many opportunities for formal training and, of course, on-the-job training.

On-the-job training
For the new translator starting work in one of the institutions, this practical training received from colleagues and revisers is the most obvious and (one hopes) the most useful training in how to translate in an institutional context. Most organisations provide all new translators with a **mentor** or "official friend"

to help them with fairly obvious problems such as how to find the canteen, how to use the archives and computer applications, how to join an orchestra or football club ... and how to cope with revisers. Revisers are probably the bane of the new translator's life. Many new translators, even experienced ones, will be taken aback by the amount of red ink that appears on their first few translations.

This is the best advice we can give to new translators starting work in the EU institutions: You must adopt a constructive attitude. First of all, you must ensure that the reviser shows you the corrections and explains them to you. Normally, they have a duty to do so. If they forget, insist politely or appeal to a third party such as your mentor or head of unit.

There are two ways in which translators can help revisers and create a good impression:

1. Leave enough time for revision. Don't hang on to the translation until just before the deadline.
2. Append a list (and/or margin notes or on-screen "comments") to show exactly which sources you have used for certain terms or quotations. Even if you've got them wrong, this shows thoroughness.

Be prepared for revisers to contradict each other – or to appear to do so. New translators often find it difficult to produce translations in different registers, and this can lead to problems when they are told to translate the French expression *décharge du budget* as "budget discharge" on Monday and as "signing off the budget" on Tuesday. The explanation is as follows: A great deal of EU material is "self-referential", that is, it involves references to earlier EU documents for which an official translation already exists. Glossaries, archives and computer tools will help you to find these earlier translations. Some earlier official translations may seem very odd, but it is best to re-use them if you are translating a legal or official text. If, however, you are translating a more informal document or one for outside readers, it may be better to use a more common expression, or to refer to "the so-called budget discharge (the official term for signing off the budget)", or even, in a more informal context, "signing off the budget (or what EU insiders call *the budget discharge*)".

But always remember that you are translating for the reader, not the reviser. Revisers are not infallible. If you disagree about a translation solution, the best way to decide is often to consult a third party, preferably a target reader.

Here is an injection of typical translator humour on the subject of revisers:

A TRANSLATION CEREMONY FOR WORDS

Dearly beloved, we are gathered here in front of our dictaphones and with the help of our typists to join together these words in perfect translation.

> Translation is an honourable occupation, instituted at the time of Europe's infancy because of the mystical union that is betwixt her member states.
>
> It is therefore not in any way to be enterprised nor taken in hand lightly or wantonly, out of lust for huge salaries, but reverently, soberly and in the fear of [insert name of Director-General], duly considering the causes for which translation was instituted.
>
> It was instituted for the proliferation of documents, and for the mutual understanding that one official might have of another.
>
> Do you, verb, perfect tense, take this feminine noun, third person singular, to be your preceding direct object? Will you take upon your past participle the appropriate feminine ending and keep to this object so long as your sentence shall last?
>
> If any Reviser can show any just cause why these words may not grammatically be joined together, let him now use his red pen or else hereafter forever hold his peace.
>
> Forasmuch, then, as these words agree together according to grammar's own laws, as evidenced by the giving and receiving of endings, I pronounce them into this microphone in perfect translation.
>
> What, therefore, this translator hath joined together let no reviser put asunder! Amen.

(Author: David Monkcom, English Translation, European Commission)

Computer training

Now that every translator is issued with a PC, the most common form of training – as for all staff – is computer training. Even if you arrive with a good knowledge of the main applications, you can be sure that the IT department will introduce a new improved operating system or e-mail software as soon as using the old one has become second nature.

Language training

Like all international organisations with a multinational staff, the EU institutions provide language training in all the official languages. Language labs are available but rarely used; most language classes are of the traditional type with about 10 pupils and a poorly paid teacher employed by a company that has been awarded a service contract to provide language teaching to the institutions. Although many EU officials need to learn languages for professional purposes (as do translators, interpreters and administrators who are required to become "the specialist on Sweden", for example), there is no distinction between training for social purposes and training for professional purposes. All language training is interinstitutional, that is, staff from all institutions can attend. It is generally assumed that it takes four years to learn a language on a standard course (two

120-minute lessons per week). More intensive courses are also available. About five years before a new country joins the EU, language courses start to be organised for the new language, usually restricted at this stage to staff who need to learn it for professional reasons (mainly translators and interpreters).

In their first year with the EU institutions, new translators are not encouraged to learn a new language but instead to consolidate their knowledge of the two or three languages with which they were recruited. Thereafter, the picture changes. In all institutions, English and French translators will be put under pressure to increase their range, because English and French are the information languages for incoming texts and also the pivot languages for translation between less common languages: Greek into Finnish, for example, can be handled by translating Greek into English and then English into Finnish, if there is enough time. When deciding on language-training priorities, it is difficult to treat all translators equally; the "interests of the service" have to come first. It obviously makes sense for an English translator to learn Latvian, because there will be plenty of demand to translate Latvian into English; but for a Spanish translator it will be less useful, as there will be little or no demand to translate Latvian into Spanish, and the few pages requested can be handled by using English as a pivot. All language learning involves an investment of money, time and energy – not least by the student – and it is frustrating to learn a difficult language which you cannot then use.

There has never yet been a shortage of translators willing to learn new languages, despite the fact that there are no financial incentives (no pay bonuses or faster promotion). In fact the opportunity to translate out of six or seven foreign languages, and to learn new ones, seems to be one of the attractions of the EU institutions. Translators just enjoy learning languages!

One language not to be forgotten (literally) is the translator's mother tongue. Almost all translators in Brussels and Luxembourg are, by definition, living outside their home country, many with a social life conducted in a language that is not their mother tongue. The danger of deterioration in one's mother-tongue skills is a real one. The best ways to counteract this are the obvious ones: reading a daily paper in one's mother tongue, watching TV programmes and films, staying in touch via the Internet. Over the years, it also helps if one can develop a more analytical way of reading: not just absorbing the information, but consciously studying how the author or journalist presents it. In our official training programmes, the need is recognised. "Refresher training in the mother tongue" is an official category of training for translators, but very little exists to meet the need. Where such training can be organised, it is usually in the form of lectures by journalists and other visiting specialists. If training providers such as universities were to develop special courses for this purpose, the EU institutions would certainly be interested.

Subject training

This is a general heading for the very wide range of training available to all in-house staff in subjects such as law, economics and EU affairs, and techniques such as management, rapid reading and administrative drafting. The translation services themselves also arrange special translator-oriented training based on suggestions made by staff.

This usually takes the form of lectures or two-day seminars. There are also some longer courses, such as the following ones at the European Commission:

- special introductory courses for new staff (Commission staff spend one week at the College of Europe in Bruges, Belgium);
- one or two-week courses in the national capitals ("Familiarisation with the Member States") about the government and administration of the host country, organised by civil servants from that country. Access to these courses is very limited, but on the rare occasions when translators have been able to take part, the courses have been much appreciated. As with all training, one of the main benefits perceived is the opportunity for contact with colleagues who are not translators.

All training during working hours has to be "in the interests of the service". Although training is officially encouraged and indeed compulsory, it has to be combined with the obligation to provide translations, and sometimes there is a conflict between the two. Naturally, translation always wins.

Job prospects for in-house translators

Career development

In most EU institutions, translators have the status of "EU officials" (French: *fonctionnaires européens*) and they are employed in the "LA" (linguistic) category on the same basis as administrators in the "A" category, and with the same pay scale. The A and LA categories are open only to applicants with a university degree or equivalent. The lowest entry grade is A8, or LA8 for linguists, intended for recent graduates with no professional experience. In practice most recruitment is at the next grade up, A7 (LA7 for linguists) for new recruits with at least three years' relevant professional experience. The normal career progression from LA8 to LA4 takes twenty years. The grades above A4/LA4 are for the lucky (?) few who take up management posts. The highest grade in the LA category is LA3. The A category also has the senior management grades A2 (Director) and A1 (Director-General). Linguists who are appointed Director or Director-General are automatically transferred to the A category.

Promotion may be slow, but job security is excellent. After an initial nine-month trial period, EU officials are employed for life. Staff salaries are high.

The basic starting salary, and the salary at the highest grade normally accessible, are:

Starting salary –   A8/LA8:   €3670
20 years later –   A4/LA4:   €6766
(before deduction of tax and addition of allowances).

Contrary to popular belief, EU officials do pay tax. But it is a special EU tax, not a national tax, and it is deducted at source, at a rate ranging from 8% to 45% depending on the official's family status and salary level. (Source of figures: Staff Regulations, latest figures quoted in COM (1999) 650, on Europa – search for "officials' salaries").

By way of comparison, a freelance translator translating 150 pages per month at the average rate of €40 per page would earn €6000 per month before tax. The freelance rate of €40 per page is an average for the whole of the European Union, where lower-end rates vary from €25 for translation into Italian to €65 for translation into Danish.

Alternatives

A permanent diet of translation and revision does not suit everyone. There are some linguists who enjoy translation so much that they do more of it in the evenings and even continue after they have retired. Others find that they need to try alternative jobs, perhaps involving more freedom of action or "responsibility". It is interesting to note, however, that once the routine of day-to-day translation has been broken, many translators find it very difficult to get back into the routine, especially if their real reason for abandoning translation in the first place was that they found it too difficult or too boring. So it is that movement away from translation is usually not reversed, although in theory it is reversible.

Support services

The alternatives that are available in the translation services of the EU institutions are, firstly, work in the "support services" of the translation service. These are the units specialising in terminology, training, freelance administration and the development of computer applications for linguists. The smaller translation services do not have separate units for this purpose, but may have one or two colleagues specialising in these areas alongside their translation work. The most genuinely "linguistic" of these areas is terminology work; terminologists provide back-up for translators by producing glossaries, validating entries in online terminology bases, researching special areas, and providing a language helpdesk that is much appreciated. When ten translators are all translating the same text (into ten different languages) it often makes sense for a single terminologist to help with the research work, and to record the findings systematically. Terminologists and documentalists can also play an important part in the pre-processing of texts suited for semi-automatic translation (for example, by automatic retrieval of certain sections from a multilingual database such as CELEX), and in providing coordinated electronic documentation prior to translation.

Management

Another alternative to full-time translation is management; it is generally felt that the translation units are best run by people who have worked as translators themselves. Heads of translation unit are often required to translate and revise, or to arbitrate between translator and reviser, so it is really not possible to do this job properly without the necessary skill and translation experience. Naturally, with a promotion system based largely on seniority and length of service as in most civil services, it takes some time to become a head of unit or head of division (at least fifteen years from recruitment at grade LA7). So management is a longer-term alternative to routine translation work. It also involves the usual frustrations of red tape, lengthy meetings, and a feeling of powerlessness, caught between the grass roots and senior management.

Transfer to administration

It is also possible for translators to move out of pure translation work into "administration" – the parallel category of graduate staff in the institutions. Most administrators are generalists, and translators are perfectly well qualified to do such jobs; moreover, some translators have specialist qualifications in law, engineering, medicine and so on, and are therefore able to compete for specialist jobs in those fields. The process of transfer from translation to administration is known as *décloisonnement* (departitioning). There is a regular trickle of translators leaving the translation services, especially at the European Parliament and the Commission – it is less common elsewhere. Translators are required to stay at least two years in the translation service before applying for a transfer. In theory, transfers can take place in the opposite direction too – administrators can be transferred into the translation services; but for some unfathomable reason this hardly ever happens. For similarly obscure reasons, former translators rarely return to translation once they have tasted the heady brew of administration.

The future

It is always unwise to make predictions, but there are a number of future trends that can be detected even without a crystal ball. In this section we outline three trends which are likely to become more pronounced in the future.

Interinstitutional cooperation

There are several reasons why it is preferable for each institution to have its own translation service: this arrangement protects confidentiality, permits faster service, and ensures that the translators understand the subject matter and background of the texts they are translating – a prerequisite for high-quality translation. It also means that they are always available to serve the needs of their own institution, and the smaller institutions do not have to fear taking fourth or fifth place after the larger and more demanding ones. It has also been argued that merging all the separate translation services into a single one would create a service so large and unwieldy that it would be difficult to manage. There would probably be no perceptible advantages, and there would certainly be diseconomies of scale.

Nevertheless, there are some areas where the different translation services in Brussels and Luxembourg can and do work together to generate true economies of scale: in the areas of training, recruitment, freelance translation, new translation tools and terminology.

Training in languages and other work-related fields is clearly an area where pooling of resources gives good results. Some language courses can only be organised if there are sufficient people willing to take part (usually a minimum of eight), and it is much easier to find eight participants for a semi-intensive course in Polish, level three, if you trawl through all the institutions in Brussels (or Luxembourg). When lecturers come to give talks on translation-related topics, translators from all the institutions in that location will be invited to listen (space permitting). This is in fact one of the most common ways in which translators from the different institutions come to meet and compare notes about their respective workplaces.

Recruitment and **freelance translation** are both areas where the institutions are fishing in a large pool of outside talent – the "market" of potential new recruits, and the freelance translation market. It makes sense for the institutions to do this in unison, as the alternative is a costly waste of effort both for us and for people in these outside markets. For example, imagine that each of the nine translation services were to hold its own recruitment examinations for the new Hungarian translators that we will all need in a few years' time. The bemused applicants, uncertain where to apply, would fill in nine complicated application forms and take nine different exams; we would need many more meetings to screen all the applications and prepare all the tests (see Chapter 3), many more markers and many more interviews at the oral examination stage. Often, the same applicants would appear on several different short-lists, thus distorting the picture of the true availability of potential new recruits. We know this, because that was the way things used to be done.

Since the 1980s, however, it has been normal for the following institutions to cooperate on recruitment: the European Parliament, the Commission, the Court of Auditors, the Economic and Social Committee and the Committee of the Regions.

The Court of Justice has special requirements – its translators must have a legal qualification – so it holds its own recruitment competitions, but shares the successful candidates with the Legal-Linguistic services of the other institutions.

The Council of the European Union also goes it alone on recruitment, as it requires all its translators to have an excellent knowledge of French and English, and recently also of a third foreign language.

The European Central Bank, the European Investment Bank and the Translation Centre all recruit directly, to meet their specific needs, usually not on the basis of the large competitive examinations that are a standard feature of recruitment to the European Parliament, Council, Commission, Committees and Courts (for more details see Chapter 3).

Holding "interinstitutional competitive examinations", as they are called, is common sense. But it is not without problems. Doing justice to each institution's special needs is not always easy, and the most problematic task is dividing up the spoils: sharing out the short-list between several institutions in a way that meets each service's needs and also takes account of the candidates' preferences, which are often very hazy at this stage.

Freelance translation is another area where it makes sense for the institutions to cooperate, and they already do so to a certain extent. The European Parliament has held joint calls for tender with the Commission and with the Translation Centre; some institutions such as the Court of Auditors and the Council simply channel their freelance translation requests through the Translation Centre. Although the EU institutions' translation services understand the need to present a united front in their dealings with freelance translators – again, for reasons of image, rationalisation of effort and convenience for our freelance contractors – we are up against a simple, insoluble problem. Each institution would really like to have exclusive access to its own dedicated freelance translators, at all times. But freelance translators don't want to be owned; they want to be **free**: free to choose their clients, free to say "no" to jobs that seem uninteresting and deadlines that are impossible, and free to say "yes" to a client who offers to pay more per page. And in this area too, each institution has special needs: the Court of Justice needs freelance translators with legal expertise, the Commission covers many technical areas (transport, new technology, medicine, food safety, radiation protection, etc.), the Banks obviously need freelance translators with a banking and financial specialisation, and so on.

Terminology is another field where interinstitutional cooperation is a reality. For many years there have been informal meetings between the various institutions' terminology specialists, to share their findings and avoid re-inventing the wheel too many times. Because of different computer infrastructures, each major institution has had to develop its own online terminology bank over the past 25 years (EUTERPE at the European Parliament, Eurodicautom at the Commission and TIS at the Council). Now, though, there is a new project, dubbed IATE (Interagency Terminology Exchange) under which all these will be merged into a single base.

The **Interinstitutional Translation Committee** brings together the heads of the various institutions' translation services, most of whom are Directors or Directors-General. It meets regularly and has a number of subcommittees discussing special areas such as workload statistics (including a standard method for page counting), freelance translation arrangements, terminology and other areas of common interest.

Field offices

The European Commission is the only institution that has so far experimented with decentralised translation in "field offices" (French: *antennes*) far away from Brussels and Luxembourg. Since 1992 the European Commission's translation service has had small field offices in several national and regional capitals, in all the Member States except for those nearest to Brussels and Luxembourg. In all the other Member States, there are one or two translators attached to the Commission's Representations; the latter serve as EU information offices in the Member States, often functioning alongside information offices for the European Parliament.

At the time of writing these small field offices exist in:
Austria (Vienna)
Denmark (Copenhagen)
Finland (Helsinki)
Germany (Berlin)
Greece (Athens)
Italy (Milan)
Portugal (Lisbon)
Spain (Madrid)
Sweden (Stockholm)

Translators are seconded there for a three-year period (another alternative to routine translation in Brussels and Luxembourg) and are at the disposal of the Head of Commission Representation for various duties such as presentations, public information, or even speechwriting. They must, however, spend a high proportion of their time on translation or other work relevant to the translation service.

Another form of field office has been used too, experimentally. In 1995, just after the accession of Finland and Sweden to the EU, large field offices were set up in Helsinki and Stockholm. They were designed to provide additional temporary translation capacity for a period of 18 months, until sufficient permanent staff had been recruited in Brussels and Luxembourg. Then they were closed down. When they were in operation, these large field offices each had approximately 25 temporary translators and 5 secretaries, with a "management" staff of 3-5 permanent translators from Brussels and Luxembourg. The experiment showed that with careful organisation and a good computer infrastructure, it was possible to translate perfectly adequately without being resident in Brussels or Luxembourg. Naturally, the temporary staff had to be hand-picked (nearly all of them subsequently became permanent officials, having passed the entrance exam either before or after their recruitment to the large field offices). They had to tolerate the sort of administrative delays and red-tape obstacles that are taken for granted in Brussels; and the experiment was fiercely opposed by the staff unions, and indeed by many translators fearful of a threat to the *status quo*. One disadvantage of the formula was that the staff were all of the same nationality and had little or no direct contact with colleagues of other nationalities. The EU institutions are multinational, so this is a fair criticism. However, this defect could easily be corrected in future field offices by having a bigger mix of nationalities (for example, if translators of other nationalities were to work at the field offices on temporary training assignments).

The outcome of the experiment was such that a high-level inspection report recommended:
a) creating similar large field offices when new Member States join the EU in the future;
b) enlarging the small field offices in the present Member States;
c) setting up field offices in all the Member States that do not yet have one.

It is clear that in future, the field office formula may become more attractive, and not only to provide temporary additional capacity for new Member States. It offers a solution to many problems.
*   The translation services, especially that of the Commission, are already large and could double in size with the next enlargements. They would benefit from being divided into smaller entities with a wider geographical spread.
*   In some countries it is difficult to recruit translators of the right calibre; it

would be easier to attract them if they did not have to move to Brussels or
Luxembourg.

- If translators are immersed in the culture of the Member States, they are
  closer to the end users of translations. This may sometimes be more important than being close to the originators of the texts in Brussels.
- The field offices provide an ideal training location for translators learning
  the language of the host country; they can continue to work at a distance for
  their "home unit" and attend language courses at the same time.
- Translation as a career would be more interesting if it included the option of
  working in other national capitals, in a management or training capacity.
- Field offices can (and already do, where they exist) provide on-the-spot
  support and documentation for local freelance translators.

Teleworking

As freelance translators and field offices have demonstrated, translations can
be produced perfectly well outside Brussels and Luxembourg, as long as central translation services exist to provide the necessary support and coordination.
The general trend towards teleworking (also referred to as distance working
and home working) will affect us too. Cost-conscious administrators see definite advantages in being able to save office space and infrastructure costs if
translators can be persuaded to work from home. Two institutions have already
put teleworking on a formal footing: the Court of Auditors has one sixth of its
staff working from home in Luxembourg; the European Parliament set up a
scheme in 1995 under which about three translators per language (less than
10%) are allowed to work at home.

Despite the feasibility and the presumed advantages, there are some problems that make teleworking less attractive for permanent translation staff.

- Under the present Staff Regulations, which lay down our terms of employment, permanent staff must live close to Brussels or Luxembourg so that
  they can be called into the office at short notice. Really distant working, in
  Crete or Lapland – or even London or Paris – is not possible under these rules.
- Translation entails online access to translation tools at all times; some of
  these are only available in-house and cannot be accessed via public networks;
  so home-working translators do not have the same computer support as those
  working in office premises. The cost of providing an exactly equivalent computer environment for home workers may well be prohibitive.
- Translation can be a solitary job and some human contact with fellow translators and other colleagues is desirable.
- For certain nationalities, translation is a predominantly female profession.
  Some fear that the hard-won right to "go out to work" will be lost if one is

expected to "stay at home and work": looking after children, preparing meals, and doing full-time translation work as well.

It is clear that teleworking will become more widespread, but given these drawbacks (especially the dangers of isolation and inadequate computer support, which are less marked with field offices), one hopes that home working will always be on a purely voluntary and limited basis.

Exercises for students

6. What the job involves

6.1 Research
6.1.1 Visit the website of a national or international translators' association (or read their printed material) and find out what they say about freelance translation rates.
6.1.2 What are the basic differences (in content) between CELEX and EUR-Lex?

6.2 Terminology
6.2.1 Do some searches in JIAMCATT and Eurodicautom (both available on the Internet, as mentioned in this chapter). Compare the results found in each when searching for a set of related terms in two languages (e.g. "teleworking", "home working" and "distance working").
6.2.2 Do some full-text searching on the Internet for the same set of related terms. Where do you find better definitions? In the terminology bases or in full text? Where do you find better translations?

6.3 Translation
6.3.1 Try your hand at typical translator humour as shown in "A TRANSLA-TION CEREMONY FOR WORDS" in Chapter 6. Translate this into another language, retaining the parallels with the Christian marriage ceremony that it parodies.
6.3.2 Try your hand at revision. Revise a fellow student's translation and get them to revise yours. What (if anything) do you learn from this?

6.4 Tools
6.4.1 Obtain a raw machine translation out of your second language into your mother tongue. Try to post-edit it (a) minimally, to make it acceptable, and (b) fully, to make it indistinguishable from a human translation. Compare the types of changes you make and the amount of time it takes.

6.4.2 Use any terminology retrieval tool at your disposal (dictionary, Internet, full text) to find some equivalents in other languages of the term "birdstrike statistics" mentioned in this chapter.

6.5   Debate

6.5.1 Do *you* think it is a good idea for translators to work from home, rather than in an office environment? Outline the advantages and disadvantages as *you* see them.

6.5.2 In this chapter we suggest that proximity to the end users of translators is sometimes more important than proximity to the authors. What do *you* think?

7. EU enlargement: what it means for translation

Enlargement: translation facts and figures

Defending multilingualism

With every new enlargement of the European Union to include new member countries, critical noises are made about our language policy, which gives small countries the "privilege" of having their language elevated to the status of an official and working language of the European institutions.

With every new enlargement, too, the EU has upheld the right to multilingualism, a solution that makes greater sense, culturally and democratically, than the more simplistic alternatives. Well-intentioned but misinformed outsiders sometimes suggest that "adopting a single language would save the taxpayer a fortune" – but, as explained in Chapter 1, the cost of multilingualism is lower than is often assumed. In actual fact the total cost of translation and interpreting in the EU institutions is currently less than €2 per year for each member of the EU's population (hardly "a fortune"!). This will not increase much with enlargement, because there is always a corresponding increase in the population.

The *raison d'être* of multilingualism is that it should not be apparent to the European person-in-the-street. For the banker in London, the EU is a political animal that speaks fluent English ... yet at the same time, a farmer in Crete can communicate with the EU institutions as if they spoke only Greek. Looked at this way, from the average citizen's point of view, the EU institutions are monolingual. That is what makes them unique among international organisations. (Not to mention this secondary benefit: the EU institutions can speak to a large proportion of the world's population in their own language – English, French, Spanish and Portuguese are all world languages too.)

So, at the language level, preparing for enlargement simply means making the necessary arrangements to enable the EU institutions to communicate in, say, Hungarian – and only Hungarian – with the Hungarian citizens who will become citizens of the EU.

It might seem like a nightmare to work with all eleven languages – or with 23 or more languages in the future – but it is simply a matter of organisation. The EU institutions have shown that they can function reasonably well despite these constraints. Organising translation for the enlarged EU is admittedly more straightforward than organising interpreting. Competent interpreters are even more difficult to find than competent translators, and interpreters have to be proficient from day one. An incompetent interpreter is more visible than an incompetent translator: poor translations can be revised, but poor interpretation can't.

For translation, coping with enlargement means finding enough well-trained translators and having a well-organised system of workflow, with maximum use of machine aids and discipline on the part of translation requesters (write less, more clearly, and plan ahead to allow enough time for translation). For interpreters, though, there is the serious technical and architectural constraint of interpreting booths. Very few meeting rooms can accommodate 11 interpreting teams, let alone 21 or more in the future. In a future scenario with 21 official languages, **full interpretation** (out of all languages into all languages) would require a team of 105 interpreters for just one meeting. There would have to be five interpreters in each of the 21 booths, each working from four different source languages. But most booths are designed to hold only three interpreters, so the conditions would be impossible. It is clear that full interpretation will have to be restricted to the highest-level meetings, such as plenary sessions of the European Parliament and ministerial meetings. Even then, it will depend on interpretation via **pivot languages** (for example, providing "Polish into Greek" by interpreting from Polish into English, and then from English into Greek). There is also the possibility of asymmetric systems such as SALT (Speak All, Listen Three) where meeting participants can speak any official language, but will have to listen to interpretation into three languages only: English, French and German.

Enlargement dates

The history of enlargements looks like this:

1950s: The founding countries were Belgium, France, Germany, Italy, Luxembourg and the Netherlands.

1973: First enlargement: Denmark, Ireland and the United Kingdom joined. Norway prepared to join, but did not do so because its people voted against membership in a referendum.

1981: Greece joined.

1986: Portugal and Spain joined.

1995: Austria, Finland and Sweden joined. Norway prepared to join, but did not do so because its people voted against membership in a referendum.

2000: Negotiations are in hand for the accession of 12 new countries with 12 new languages, and the institutions are preparing to work in 23 official languages.

The applicant countries are Bulgaria, Cyprus, the Czech Republic, Estonia, Hungary, Latvia, Lithuania, Malta, Poland, Romania, Slovakia and Slovenia.

In Malta, English and Maltese are the official languages, and Maltese can take precedence over English in certain circumstances. Cyprus is officially a bilingual country with Greek and Turkish as its official languages. Greek is already an official EU language, but Turkish is not.

Pre-accession and post-accession needs

Translation of the *acquis communautaire* (EU legislation in force)

As explained in Chapter 1, some EU legislation is directly applicable in the Member States, and their citizens must be able to read and understand it in order to comply with it. That naturally includes the new Member States. Many thousands of pages of legislation have been created since the beginnings of the EU in the 1950s, and all of the legislation still in force has to be:
- translated into the official languages of any countries that join the EU,
- revised by the EU institutions,
- published in a Special Edition of the Official Journal on the day of accession.

The components of the *acquis communautaire* are:
(a) primary legislation (the Treaties)
and
(b) secondary legislation derived from the Treaties (called the *droit dérivé* in French)
and
(c) case law of the Court of Justice.

Before a new Member State can join the EU, the primary and secondary legislation, and the most important parts of the case law, have to be translated.

Translation into the new languages is the responsibility of the governments of the countries applying for membership. It is usually done in the national Ministry of Justice, Ministry of Foreign Affairs or Ministry for European Integration, or in a translation centre created for the purpose. The translations have to be revised by the EU institutions so that they can be authenticated and published as "equally authentic" versions of EU legislation in the Official Journal. On the day of accession, they become official versions of EU legislation, in the same way as the existing German, Italian and Finnish versions. In some of the countries now applying for membership, translation of the *acquis* began in 1996, with technical assistance from the Commission. Each applicant country has set up a special unit to translate the *acquis* into the national language. These units are usually known as TCUs (Translation Coordination Units) and their structure and funding vary. They have all been aided by the Commission's TAIEX office (Technical Assistance Information Exchange). TAIEX has also been responsible for obtaining translations into English or French of those parts of the national legislation which need to be monitored by the Commission officials checking on the conformity of national law with EU legislation (the process known as **screening**). TAIEX has an interesting website with up-to-date information at <http://cadmos.carlbro.be>.

Translating the *acquis* has been described as "the linguistic equivalent of climbing Mount Everest". Simply translating the Treaties is a major task, more because of their fundamental importance than because of the number of pages involved. But translating the secondary legislation in force is a massive undertaking, demanding a sustained effort that must be based on sound linguistic, terminological and technical input. At the last enlargement in 1995, the Finnish and Swedish Special Editions of the Official Journal containing the *acquis* were each nearly 50 000 pages long. Fifty thousand OJ pages are equivalent to more than 100 000 standard A4 pages of 1500 characters.

Doubts are often expressed as to whether the applicant countries, especially the smaller ones, will be able to finish the translation work in time. This is not new – it happened in the past too, with countries that are now full members of the EU. It is reassuring to note that some of the smaller applicant countries, such as Estonia and Slovenia, are in fact the furthest advanced in the translation work. And this despite the fact that it is much easier to find the necessary number of translators, revisers and legal experts to do this work in a large population than in a small one.

It is not unusual for small countries to attach greater importance to their national language than do larger countries, and therefore to give higher priority to translating EU legislation. For them, joining the European Union means that, for the very first time, their citizens, their Members of the European Parliament and their national ministers will be able to speak their national language in international meetings far away from their home country.

The daunting task of translating the *acquis* is probably the only one in the entire accession operation that is exactly the same, in both quantitative and qualitative terms, for every would-be Member State. But this major translation project is straightforward compared with the wider efforts being demanded of these countries to adapt to EU membership, in areas such as institution building, democratic structures and the creation of competitive market economies.

Revising the translations of primary and secondary legislation

In the final phase of the membership negotiations, the translations of the *acquis* produced in the applicant countries are revised by the institutions. The revision work is traditionally shared by the Council and the Commission.

This is not intended as a criticism of the work done by the applicant countries. Revision is carried out for the simple reason that the institutions have an obligation to ensure that every language version, starting with the Treaties, is in agreement and can be published as an "authentic language version". The decisions taken by legal experts at this stage, especially as regards terminology and conventional phrasing, must then be applied consistently in all the translations so that they are legally watertight.

In earlier enlargements, this revision work was carried out in Brussels by revisers recruited from the applicant countries. But last time round, a different formula was tried: part of the revision was done in the applicant countries, by *ad hoc* teams of revisers employed by the Commission and attached to the Commission's Delegations in Finland, Norway and Sweden. (No revision team was required in Austria, as German was already an official language). This new formula was tried partly because it was easier to recruit qualified staff if they did not have to move to Brussels, and partly because actual membership was uncertain – it depended on national referenda held a few months before the planned date of accession, and the translation and revision work had to start long before that! In the end, Norway decided not to join the EU, and the revision work in the Oslo Revision Office was duly halted.

This formula was only possible thanks to new technology and telecommunications, and it will probably be repeated for future enlargements. One of the major advantages is that of proximity to the national unit that produced the translations of the *acquis* and the opportunity for feedback and close cooperation. It is also useful to have a team of translators on the spot who can build up contacts with national universities and professional associations, and thus create networks for information on recruitment of future translators for the EU institutions.

In-house preparation for enlargement

In the run-up to expected enlargements, the translation services of the EU institutions and bodies all have to prepare to provide translations *out of* the new languages that will become official languages when new countries join. These new translation demands are normally met by training existing staff to translate out of more languages, and training has to start well before the new countries join. Learning a language takes several years, but translators always welcome the opportunity to add new languages to their portfolio, and this willingness is exploited to the full. Since 1996, some 150 translators at the Commission (and proportionally equivalent numbers in the other institutions) have been taking courses in Czech, Estonian, Hungarian, Polish and Slovene. Courses in the languages of the other applicant countries are in preparation. Translators are also encouraged to attend intensive courses in the countries concerned.

However, there will be one difference with the next enlargements. It is no longer reasonable to expect translators to translate out of *all* the official languages. Eight or nine foreign languages seem to be the maximum any translator can absorb. With the next enlargement we will have to consider a change of approach. For the first time, some of the EU translation services (including the Commission's) are considering abandoning the "mother tongue" principle, whereby translators translate only into their mother tongue. Instead they are planning to introduce "**two-way translation**" (*traduction aller-retour* in French), so called because translators will be allowed to translate in two directions: *into* and *out of* their mother tongue. So translators recruited from the new Member States will normally translate into their mother tongue, in accordance with the standard and most logical practice, but may be required also to translate out of their mother tongue into English or French. Two-way translation will be used only if the texts are for internal information and are not intended for publication or outside distribution.

Apart from providing language training, the translation services have to prepare for enlargement by adapting their computer systems and computer-aided translation tools to cope with new languages. The software and hardware such as keyboards must be able to support the alphabets and accented characters of the new languages. These problems will be minor compared with the great challenge that had to be met in 1981, when computer systems were far less sophisticated than they are today: that of integrating the Greek alphabet.

A very important area is terminology development. When the translators start work in Brussels and Luxembourg, translating into the new languages after the accession of a new country, they must have well-stocked and reliable terminology bases, and these can only be created by close collaboration from an early stage with the translation centres in each applicant country.

A decade ago, the only equipment most translators had was a dictaphone, but things have changed. In all the EU institutions' translation services, translators now have access to a full range of new computer technology; and ideally the full range of new tools – such as voice recognition, translation memories and machine translation – must be prepared or developed for the new languages as well.

We also need to prospect the freelance market for translators proficient in the new languages (as source or target) and arrange calls for tender to build up our freelance lists.

Recruitment

Recruitment of translators is the most important part of preparing the translation services for enlargement. Taken together, the institutions will need more than 200 translators for each language (not including interpreters).

As explained elsewhere in this book, the different institutions have different needs. The Court of Justice needs translators with a legal qualification as well as excellent languages. The European Parliament, Economic and Social Committee and Committee of the Regions, and also the Court of Justice, will be looking for translators capable of translating out of *any of the official languages*;

while the Commission's and Council's prime need is for translators able to translate out of *French and English*, which are the main drafting languages in those institutions. For the first time, we will also be seeking translators who are, in addition, able to translate out of their mother tongue into English or French ("two-way" translation for information purposes, as mentioned above).

Despite the differences between the institutions' requirements, most of them worked together in 1994, 1995 and 1996 in joint "interinstitutional" competitions to recruit the Finnish and Swedish translators needed for the last accession.

The "enlargement" competitions are identical to all other recruitment competitions as regards conditions of access (age limits, qualifications required, types of tests, etc.). These are described in Chapter 3 of this book.

Universities offering translation courses in the applicant countries are encouraged to contact the EU institutions. The Commission's TAIEX office arranges study visits and Round Tables on many topics – see their website at <http://cadmos.carlbro.be>. The translation services themselves have received numerous trainees from the applicant countries, who have been taken on for short periods, usually by the terminology department, with a view to training them in our working methods and generally to acquaint them with the operation of the translation services.

In a nutshell

To summarise the above, there are:

- pre-accession translation needs (the translation and revision of the *acquis*);
- post-accession translation needs:
    translation **out of** new languages (the training of existing staff);
    translation **into** new languages (the recruitment of new translators).

However, these activities occur concurrently, not consecutively, over a period of several years before actual accession, as shown below. The year "X" is the year of accession.

	PRE-ACCESSION		POST-ACCESSION	
	year X - 4	year X - 1	year X	year X + 1
Acquis	Translation starts in national ministries or TCUs.	We start to revise and authenticate*. From September, preparation for Special Edition of OJ.	Special Edition of OJ published; *acquis* becomes national law.	Business as usual.
Translation **out of** new languages	We start training our in-house translators.	We continue training.	We start translating out of the new languages.	Business as usual.
Translation **into** new languages	Training in universities.	We hold exams for recruitment.	We recruit the first translators for the new languages.**	We continue recruiting until business can run as usual.

* The primary legislation (Treaties) should be authenticated in year X - 2.
** Occasionally it is possible to recruit new staff on a temporary basis in year X - 1.

A virtual accession: Newland joins the EU

In this section we describe the challenges facing an imaginary country, which we call "Newland", in the various stages of translation work linked to accession. Let's call Newland's national language Newlish.

At each stage we explain the mistakes to be avoided and best practice to be copied. The mistakes are of course imaginary and we do not wish to suggest that any country has made them in the past, or is making them at present. The best practices are based on reality and on new possibilities created by developments since the last accession.

Translation of the *acquis* into Newlish

This is carried out by a national ministry or Translation Coordination Unit (TCU) in the national capital.

Mistakes to be avoided
- Letting translators think that they are translating "for information only". The translations will eventually (when revised and authenticated) become part of Newland's national law. The translation choices made in the *acquis* translations will be obligatory choices in future Newlish translations of EU legislation. To some extent they will also influence the future development of Newlish, as EU terms and concepts are assimilated into the national consciousness.
- Expecting translators to work in isolation from each other. Networking and shared terminology are essential.
- Using inexperienced or badly paid translators and putting them under too much time pressure.
- Not providing legal and technical advice to solve translation problems.
- Being disorganised: doing translation in the wrong order, translating the wrong texts or translating the same thing several times over.
- Thinking that the *acquis* texts are typical of translation work in the EU institutions (they aren't).

Best practice to be copied
- Translate in the right order (the primary legislation should be translated before the secondary legislation; the basic acts that create the terminology have to be translated first, as subsequent acts re-use or quote that terminology, and certain conventions have to be created for legal phraseology).
- Cultivate national contacts who can give advice on legal and technical terminology (subject specialists and experts in national ministries).

- Set up *ad hoc* advisory committees of lawyers, translators and subject experts (on agriculture, transport, customs, etc.) to validate the translations of key pieces of legislation.
- Work with a database or translation memory to ensure consistent terminology and agreed phrasing conventions.
- Make maximum use of translation aids to ensure consistency.
- Take a positive attitude to revision. Revisers' corrections should be seen as part of the team effort, not as a personal affront.
- Accept responsibility for getting it right and don't imagine that "Brussels" can give guidance on linguistic points (It can't. It doesn't speak Newlish yet. The responsibility is Newland's. If "Brussels" appears to be imposing unnatural linguistic forms, get the Newlish lawyers to challenge them on your behalf.)

Translation out of Newlish: training of in-house staff

This is the responsibility of the EU institutions in Brussels and Luxembourg.

Mistakes to be avoided
- Leaving training courses until too late. It takes three or four years to learn a new language.
- Finishing training too early. If there is too long a wait before Newland's accession, the translators will have little chance to maintain their knowledge.
- Using non-professional language teachers. A colleague's Newlish spouse may be charming, but charm is not enough – he or she should also be qualified to teach Newlish as a foreign language. Translators are very demanding pupils.
- Over-emphasising active language skills. Passive knowledge is more important for translators.
- Expecting staff to pay for training themselves, on top of the mental effort of learning the language.

Best practice to be copied
- Providing language training specifically designed for translators.
- Providing "conversion courses" for translators who already know a related language (e.g. before Sweden joined, translators who knew Danish were given conversion courses to enable them to translate out of Swedish).
- Contacting universities in Newland for advice on language training, textbooks, etc.
- Inviting Newlish university staff to Brussels and Luxembourg to help provide training.

Translation into Newlish: training of future translators in Newland

This will take place in Newland's universities and translator training institutes.

Mistakes to be avoided
- Forgetting that translators need a university-level diploma if they are to be recruited as EU officials (usually requiring four years of study).
- Neglecting training in the mother tongue (Newlish), as translators will be required to translate into their mother tongue. Translation out of the mother tongue will be an optional extra, not a central task.
- Forgetting to learn French. French is an extremely important language in the European Union and it is also essential for social integration in Brussels and Luxembourg.
- Forgetting that translators will be expected to know at least **two** foreign languages (which must be official languages of the EU).

Best practice to be copied
- Contact the EU institutions or universities in EU countries to find out about the translator training required.
- Organise conferences and networks on the topic.
- Work together with the national translators' association(s). For example, practising translators can provide input to university courses; universities can offer lectures and courses for practising translators on translation techniques, EU language and EU institutions.

Translation into Newlish: recruitment to the EU institutions

This is always organised by the EU institutions recruiting translators.

Mistakes to be avoided
- Leaving it too late. One year before accession is the best time to start.
- Making dogmatic assumptions about the equivalence of university diplomas. Advice may be needed from Newland's Ministry of Education.
- Failing to provide information for universities and candidates.
- Giving the impression that translators will spend all their time translating legislation (as per *acquis*, above).

Best practice to be copied
- Organise interinstitutional recruitment competitions, rather than separate recruitment competitions for each institution (NB separate competitions are justified where there are special needs, e.g. for lawyer-linguists, but here

too, the competitions can be jointly organised by the Court of Justice and the three other institutions requiring lawyer-linguists).

- Contact Newland's universities for assistance with marking of test papers, and explain the criteria for assessment (e.g. that the applicants' ability to write well in their mother tongue is more important than their knowledge of foreign languages).
- Set up an information website with frequently asked questions and answers.

Public reactions in Newland to EU translations (criticism of translationese and fear that Newlish will be corrupted)

Mistakes to be avoided
- Thinking that this problem is unique to Newland.
- Automatically blaming the Newlish translators.

Best practice to be copied
- Compare Newland's experience with that of older Member States, whose language has not in fact been terminally corrupted by EU membership. Italy is a good example. Has Italy's language or culture been damaged by 50 years as a member of the EU?
- Accept that membership of the EU will inevitably introduce some new concepts that have to be named in Newlish and understood in Newland.
- Appoint a language coordinator for Newlish (in the EU institutions, and perhaps also in Newland) to deal specifically with Euro-Newlish.
- Encourage the Newlish press to print articles about translation; encourage Newlish TV to show documentaries and discussion programmes on translation and language.
- Explain to the public that texts translated into Newlish, about abstruse EU topics, are inevitably less readable than original material written in Newlish on more familiar subjects.
- Defend the newly recruited Newlish translators from unfair criticism, but don't let them get into bad habits either! Encourage them to stay in touch with real Newlish and to avoid writing in Euro-Newlish.

Exercises for students

7. EU enlargement

7.1 Research
7.1.1 Find two recent newspaper articles about EU enlargement published in the national press (paper or on-line versions):
a) one in your first foreign language

b) one in your mother tongue.

7.1.2   Access the TAIEX site mentioned in this chapter, or another official site on enlargement, and find out about the relative state of progress of two different applicant countries (for example, Poland and Bulgaria), and the probable accession dates.

7.2   Terminology

7.2.1.   Compare the two articles identified an exercise 7.1.1 and if possible produce a mini-glossary of corresponding terms used in each.

7.2.2   Has your mother tongue been influenced in any way by the existence of the EU? Find five terms in your mother tongue that did not exist before 1950, or were used in another way previously, and are attributable to the EU. Indicate sources (dictionaries used).

7.3   Translation

7.3.1   Translate all or part of the article you found for Exercise 7.1.1 a) into your mother tongue. Try to use some of the terms from the article found in Exercise 7.1.1 b).

7.3.2   Translate the first two paragraphs of Chapter 7 into your mother tongue or first foreign language. Please note: they were originally written in French. Can you tell? How?

7.4   Tools

7.4.1   Imagine you were involved in translating the *acquis* into a completely new language. Write a one-page justification for acquiring translation memory tools for this purpose.

7.4.2   Use graphics software or presentation software such as PowerPoint to produce a map of Europe with different colours to distinguish between Member States, applicant countries and non-member countries.

7.5   Debate

7.5.1   Discuss the advantages and disadvantages of what we call *two-way translation* in the "Recruitment" section of this chapter, and elsewhere in this book. Is it preferable always to translate **into** one's mother tongue? Might there be some advantages in translating **out of** one's mother tongue? What are they?

7.5.2   It has been suggested that the EU will be unable to function with more than the present eleven official languages. What do *you* think?

8. Translator and user profiles

This chapter consists of interviews with the translators, ex-translators and translation users named below, and its purpose is to show the living context of the facts presented in the earlier chapters. No attempt was made to influence the interviewees in any way; they had not read the rest of the book and they did not see the others' replies. All the views presented are personal. In some cases the views coincide with ours; in some they diverge. They also differ from each other to some extent, and thus illustrate the challenge of designing translation services that meet the needs of many translators and many clients.

We tried to include interviewees of several different nationalities and from several different institutions. We would have liked to cover all fifteen nationalities and all nine translation services, but that would have made the chapter too long. As there is no such thing as a "typical translator" or a "typical user", we chose interesting ones instead.

In each case we give a brief profile of the person interviewed, followed by special questions tailored to that person and then general questions put to all interviewees in the group. The interviews were conducted by e-mail in November and December 2000. All respondents were kind enough to reply in English, and their replies have been edited only minimally. We would like to thank them all for their contribution to this book.

EU Institutions	Translators	Users
European Parliament	Renato Da Costa Correia (Nationality: Portuguese)	Michiel van Hulten (Nationality: Dutch)
Council	Anna-Karin Batcheller (Nationality: Swedish)	Hans Brunmayr (Nationality: Austrian)
Commission	Monique Scottini (Nationality: Italian)	
	Jyrki Lappi-Seppälä (Nationality: Finnish)	David O'Sullivan (Nationality: Irish)
Court of Justice	Jesper Meyer (Nationality: Danish)	
A freelance translator	Clare Sholl (Nationality: British)	

Interviews with some translators and ex-translators

Renato da Costa Correia, translator at the European Parliament

---

Profile:

Renato da Costa Correia is Portuguese; his mother tongue is Portuguese and he also knows Dutch, English, French, German, and a little Greek, Italian, Luxembourgish and Spanish.

He is a translator at the European Parliament in Luxembourg; before that he was a lecturer at Coimbra University in Portugal and helped organise one of the first postgraduate courses for translators in his country.

In recent years he has given lectures and seminars for fellow-translators on translation theory and the history of translation. He also gives seminars on the language provisions of the European institutions for trainees at the EP Translation Service.

How much contact do translators at the European Parliament have with Members of the European Parliament? Do you have an opportunity to meet them and attend parliamentary sessions?

Apart from personal acquaintances, contacts with Members are virtually non-existent. On some rare occasions translators are given the opportunity to attend parliamentary committee meetings.

You have had an interesting career, as a university teacher of translation and now as a translator yourself. If you went back to teaching now, what (if anything) would you teach differently?

I would change neither the general approach nor the methods, but I would certainly use a wider variety of text types for practical training (e.g. legal, administrative, technical).

Do you think that translators in the EU institutions would be more effective if they knew more about translation theory?

If by effectiveness you mean awareness of general and specific translation problems and the ability to cope with them, the answer is definitely yes.

Why did you become a translator?

One day I decided to find out if the theoretical background and the methods I had passed on to a large number of students were any good, by using them myself. It has been a rewarding experience so far.

Was it a deliberate career choice?
It certainly was.

Did you have specific university training as a translator?
I didn't have any specific university training as a translator, but I did give it to quite a lot of students. Life isn't always logical, is it?

Since starting work here, have you learnt any new languages? Which ones? Was it for professional or social reasons? Were you happy with the language training provided?
I took further training in Dutch for professional reasons, taught myself some Luxembourgish for social reasons and started learning Greek out of intellectual curiosity. Language training is severely limited in its results by the fact that there are too few specific courses for translators.

What do you enjoy most about being a translator? What do you not enjoy? Would you like to change over to administration? If so, why? If not, why not?
As a translator I enjoy a large freedom of mind in an otherwise rather hierarchical and constraining environment. Odd, but true. Being an incorrigible introvert, I also like the possibility of doing teamwork without too much shoulder-rubbing. I deeply dislike the ignorance about translation often demonstrated by those who rely on translators to guarantee the effectiveness of their own work.
    As a typical specimen of *Homo philologicus*, the only tasks I would consider performing within administration would have to be connected with text drafting or with research on linguistic or societal areas.

Have you worked as a freelance translator?
No.

Can you imagine working as a freelance in future?
Yes, I can. But I don't think I'd like it.

Do you have much contact with translation requesters?
Only when I call them about translation problems.

Do you have enough information about the purpose of translations?
There is enough information available about the general purpose of translations, but not enough information about the specific purpose of individual translations.

Do you ever get feedback from end users (e.g. readers in the Member States)?
Not that I know of.

Have you ever complained about the quality of an original text? What was the response?
Occasionally. The response scale ranged from an apology and an explanation to sheer incapacity to understand the whole fuss, when everybody could see what was meant. The best compliment I've received so far was: 'Oh, I see you've read the text very carefully.'

Are there any translation-related activities, apart from actual translation, that you are able to carry out occasionally (terminology work, teaching, lecturing, training colleagues, writing guides for translators, etc.)?
Yes. See profile.

Do you think it would be a good idea to merge all the institutions' translation services into one?
No, I don't. And I don't think it's only a matter of (over)size. European institutions have different needs, as far as translation is concerned, and each of them has developed its own translation culture. The consequences of recent culture clashes resulting from company mergers should teach everybody a lesson.

Anna-Karin Batcheller, translator at the Council of the European Union

---

Profile:
Anna-Karin Batcheller is Swedish; she is bilingual in English and Swedish, and also knows French and Spanish. She passed the recruitment competitions for both Swedish and English mother-tongue translators.
  She is a junior Swedish translator at the Council of the European Union in Brussels, where she started work in September 2000. Before that she worked in Canada and Sweden as both a freelance and a staff translator.

As a newcomer to the EU institutions, how do you find them compared with your previous employment? Is it a culture shock for Swedes to work in Brussels?
I haven't found it very hard to adapt to my new working environment. A big difference is that now I have colleagues who also are translators, unlike before when I was the only one at my place of work. It is great to be able to discuss translation problems and to feel that you are part of a team. I don't think I experienced a culture shock when I came to Brussels. Almost all the people I work with are Swedish and, having spent many years abroad, I didn't expect things to be the same as "at home" anyway.

You are now a junior translator "on probation", so your work has to be revised. Do you find that difficult?

I am used to having my work revised by the teachers in the translation program I attended and by a staff translator who revised the patent translations I did as a freelance translator. I think that revision should be the norm for all translations, as a quality control measure. However, it must be based on a good relationship between translators and revisers. Cooperation and feedback are essential.

It is very unusual for applicants to pass recruitment competitions for two languages, as you have done. Congratulations! How did you do it?

I think the main reason I succeeded in the competition for English mother-tongue translators is that I lived in an English-speaking environment for fourteen years and that I have spoken English on a daily basis with my Canadian boyfriend/ husband for twenty years. I also found the English language absolutely fascinating from the moment I started learning it in school, and I have put a lot of effort into mastering it. I started reading English novels at an early age and made a point of always looking up the words I didn't know, and I still read more in English than in Swedish.

As for translating into Swedish, I worked with the language while living abroad, and the translation program I attended after moving back to Sweden gave me the professional training I needed.

Why did you become a translator? Was it a deliberate career choice? Did you have specific university training as a translator?

I always wanted to work with languages but when I first attended university there was no specific program for translators in Sweden and not much of a job market either. Later, in Canada, I started working as a freelance translator and enjoyed it very much. So when the opportunity arose to go back to Sweden to do a master's program in translation I just had to do it, even though it involved many changes not just for me but for my family as well.

Since starting work here, have you learnt any new languages? Which ones? Was it for professional or social reasons? Were you happy with the language training provided?

I haven't learned any new languages yet but I hope to start a course either in one of the "deficit" languages or one of the languages of the applicant countries in the autumn.

What do you enjoy most about being a translator? What do you not enjoy? Would you like to change over to administration? If so, why? If not, why not?

What I enjoy most is the challenge of producing a translation that is both faithful and idiomatic and to find solutions to translation problems whether they are syntactic or terminological. However, since many of the translations we do at the Council are based on previous documents, we have to do a lot of cutting and pasting, which can be a bit tedious. I only recently started working at the Council and I am still learning, so I haven't even considered working in administration. I enjoy my present job very much and at the moment I find it hard to imagine wanting to change.

Have you worked as a freelance translator? Can you imagine working as a freelance in future?
I worked part-time as a freelance translator in Canada while my children were small, and after graduating from the translation program at Lund University in 1997 I worked half-time as a staff translator and half-time as a freelance translator. The advantage of being a freelance translator is that you are more independent and can set your own working hours to some extent, although, naturally, you have to provide a timely service and there is a risk of taking on too much work once you have become established. For now I like being a staff translator.

Do you have much contact with translation requesters? Do you have enough information about the purpose of translations? Do you ever get feedback from end users (e.g. readers in the Member States)?
So far, no to all three.

Have you ever complained about the quality of an original text? What was the response?
As with any writing there can be deficiencies, whether stylistic or grammatical, but so far I have not complained about any original text.

Are there any translation-related activities, apart from actual translation, which you are able to carry out occasionally (terminology work, teaching, lecturing, training colleagues, writing guides for translators, etc.)?
Not yet, but I look forward to being able to do so in the future.

Do you think it would be a good idea to merge all the institutions' translation services into one?
I don't think I have been here long enough to be able to answer that question. But it might result in a very large organisation where the translators were too far removed from the institutions that are producing and using the texts.

Monique Scottini, ex-translator, now responsible for Electronic Document Registry in the European Commission

Profile:
Monique Scottini is Italian; her mother tongue is French and she knows English, German, Dutch, Italian, Danish, Greek, Spanish, Portuguese, and Finnish.

She was a French translator in the Commission's translation service for 16 years and has now moved to an administrative job in the Commission's Secretariat-General in Brussels. She runs the team that collates all the language versions of documents adopted by the Commission and aligns them (to ensure that they all match) before sending them for publication or to the other EU bodies (European Parliament, Council, Economic and Social Committee and so on) for further political discussion.

Can we talk first about your "former life" as a translator? Why did you become a translator?
I was both an interpreter and a translator before joining the Commission and a translator after joining the Commission. Languages have always been an important part of my life, because they are the main link that enables people to communicate. Language is one of the main features that differentiate human beings from animals.

Was it a deliberate career choice?
Yes, absolutely.

Did you have specific university training as a translator?
I had a university training as an interpreter, and I translated a medical book by Alexander Mitscherlich from German into French as my thesis. It was one of the first scientific works dealing with psychosomatic diseases.

After starting work for the Commission, did you learn any new languages? Which ones? Was it for professional or social reasons?
Yes. I learned Spanish, Portuguese, Danish and Finnish for professional reasons after starting work for the Commission. I had studied German and English at university, and I already knew Dutch, because I had learned it at secondary school. I taught myself Modern Greek; as I had done Latin and Greek at school, it was easy for me to learn Modern Greek and Italian. Moreover, my husband is Italian; I have Italian nationality and I hope to live in Italy after retirement. So learning Italian was very important for my private life.

What did you enjoy about being a translator?
To think that, thanks to my translations, people will be able to understand the meaning of the texts concerned.

What did you not enjoy?
The fact that I was not myself the writer of the original text. As a translator, you have to translate as accurately as possible even if the text is full of nonsense. I really like to write and sometimes I thought that the result would have been much better if I had been the writer of the original text rather than the translator.

Why did you change over to administration?
I think I had already given the best of myself to the Commission's Translation Service. I was able to translate from nine official languages into French. Learning another language was not a challenge any longer. Having been actively involved in three major modernisation projects in the Translation Service, including one to set up an electronic archive of all translations, I had gained other competencies which could be very useful elsewhere. I felt able to run a project and I needed new challenges. At the time the Secretariat General of the Commission was trying to "go electronic" by creating an electronic registry for all official documents. When I was offered the chance to take over this project, which had been a failure for about 11 years, I thought it was both an interesting challenge for me and a job which could be more useful to more people. Succeeding in going over from a paper registry to an electronic registry would enable everybody to have access to all official documents in all languages after adoption by the Commission. It was an important missing link for the other institutions, the citizens, and all the DGs.

Did your years in the Translation Service provide you with useful experience that you could channel into your new job?
Yes, absolutely. But translation experience alone would not have been enough, even translating from nine languages. It was the competencies and experience I had gained thanks to my involvement in the three modernisation projects that interested the Secretariat General. It is because they were convinced that I could be the leader of a major modernisation project for the whole Commission that I was offered the job.

Or did you feel at a disadvantage, perhaps, because you were "labelled" as a translator?
I think it would have been easier for me if I had left the Translation Service when I was younger. It is much more difficult for a senior translator to get a job in administration.

Now you see the Translation Service from a different point of view, what suggestions do you have? What do you think could be improved?
The Translation Service should become more responsible. It is the Directorate General with the highest percentage of officials with a university degree. Translators are very competent in language matters, but they are too shy and too passive in general. Too many translators see themselves as real experts in language and they really are excellent experts in that field, but they do not see themselves as potential managers, as people who should think and take full responsibility for the texts they produce in view of the decision-making process of the Commission. In many DGs, even C-grade secretaries have more responsibilities than translators do. I think it is very important for the future of the Translation Service that translators become active partners. There must be real added value in the service offered. Being a good service provider is not enough: service providers can just as well be private firms working for the Commission.

As a user of translations, are you satisfied with the service provided?
The quality is not homogeneous enough. Moreover, we encounter real problems with the deadlines. This is why I think that the Commission's Translation Service should become an active partner in the decision-making process. Having a text that is perfect in some languages, but not yet available in some other languages, prevents the Commission from playing the role it should play in the interinstitutional triangle. Recently, just to give you an example, we had a serious problem with one political dossier. The Council had been negotiating the whole night. It had only received the papers in English, French and German. The small countries insisted on having the translation in their own language. The Commissioner in charge had promised the Portuguese Minister that he would get the Portuguese translation the following morning. The Registry of the Commission had unfortunately been unable to deliver the text concerned the day before, because there were still some mistakes in the Portuguese translation delivered. To settle the problem, the Commissioner had to apologise publicly.

But you say the Portuguese translation had been delivered to you, so the Translation Service was not to blame for the delay. Were the mistakes linguistic or presentational?
The mistakes were of three types:
1) linguistic: the title of the proposal for a regulation had been changed during the decision-making process and the Portuguese translation did not match the new title;
2) legalistic: no numbering of the Recitals, as stipulated in the new Agreement between the Legal Services of the Commission, Council and Parliament;
3) presentational: some titles were not numbered.

It must be stressed that three different units in the DG concerned had drafted the original text of the proposal. This resulted in co-ordination problems at all stages of the procedure.

Do you think the translations are generally accurate? In style, are they too administrative-sounding? Or too "journalistic"?
I think the style is quite good in general. The problem is not there. The problem is that parts are sometimes missing, that figures and footnotes are not correct, that translators do not always use the right template for the type of decision ("decision" as opposed to "*sui generis* decision") and things like that. The electronic quality of the files could also be improved (graphs, tables, incorrect formatting codes, track changes).

What do you think is more important: delivery on time, or quality?
Delivery on time is more important, but the quality should be correct as well.

Have you ever experienced problems because translations were not available in time?
Every day, we have problems: translations not available, or corrections not returned in time to enable us to transmit the files immediately after adoption by the Commission. Here again, I think that the situation would be different if the Commission's Translation Service were an active partner in the decision-making process. Translators would work differently if they were aware of all the political problems resulting from a translation either not delivered on time or of a too poor quality to be transmitted as such to the other institutions.

Do you think that some problems arise, perhaps, because requesters of translations do not plan ahead and are then surprised that translations can't be delivered as rapidly as they would like?
Yes, it is obvious that some problems are due to a lack of planning from the requesters of translations, but it is not always easy to have perfect forward planning when you have to meet political deadlines and to consult so many services before a decision can be made at Commission level. The texts resulting from the decision-making process change so many times before being finalised that some DGs wait until the last minute to have a consolidated text before sending it for translation. Political priorities may also change, hence the need to have one text translated rather than another.

Do you ever use machine translation? What do you think of it?
I have used it from time to time, to get a first draft in English for instance. The quality is good enough to get the general meaning of the text.

Do you think the public image of the Commission is affected by translation?
Yes, the Commission's Translation Service is contributing towards the public image (good or bad) of the Commission. In that respect, it has a more political role to play than it thinks it has.

Do you think it would be a good idea to merge all the institutions' translation services into one?
I don't know. The important thing is that the Commission's Translation Service should no longer see itself as a mere service provider, but as a real partner, with a political role to play in the decision-making process of the Commission.

Jesper Meyer, legal reviser at the European Court of Justice

Profile:
Jesper Meyer is Danish; his mother tongue is Danish and he also knows English, French, German, Greek and Spanish.
  He is a legal reviser at the European Court of Justice in Luxembourg; before that he was a solicitor in a law firm in Denmark for two years after studying law at Århus University.

Why do the translators employed by the European Court of Justice have to be lawyers? Couldn't translators without legal qualifications do this work?
The texts we translate are mainly judgments of the Courts, opinions of the advocates general and requests for preliminary rulings from national courts. These texts are normally written in a special way and with special legal concepts which only lawyers are able to understand fully and reproduce in their own language. That is why the revisers and translators have to be lawyers. Sometimes we have to deviate from this principle when sending texts to freelance translators, since it is impossible to find enough lawyers for this purpose, but freelance translations are always revised by an in-house lawyer.

Your job title is "legal reviser". What is that, exactly? Is it the same as a "lawyer-linguist"? Do legal revisers translate as well as revise?
It is not quite the same, although in some language divisions the distinction has become less clear in recent years. In principle, each language division has three kinds of linguists, namely "lawyer-linguists" who (in most cases) only translate and whose work is usually revised, "principal lawyer-linguists" who translate, often without revision, and occasionally revise if necessary, and "legal revisers" who revise and occasionally translate if necessary.

People with legal qualifications and language skills must be in great demand on the job market – does the Court of Justice have difficulty finding them?
Yes, great difficulty, especially for some languages. For example, there was only one(!) successful candidate at the last competition for English lawyer-linguists.

Why did you become a translator?
Because I found it interesting to try and live abroad and because I always liked working with foreign languages (and writing in my own).

Was it a deliberate career choice?
No, it was more or less a coincidence! I was doing quite well as a lawyer and my career track seemed to be settled, when all of a sudden my brother, who was already working for the Commission at that time, sent me a copy of the *avis de concours* for Danish lawyer-linguists at the European Court of Justice. I participated more for the experience, thinking that my French was too poor anyway and that I was quite happy where I was.

Did you have specific university training as a translator?
None whatsoever.

Since starting work here, have you learnt any new languages? Which ones? Was it for professional or social reasons? Were you happy with the language training provided?
I have learnt Spanish, mostly for translation purposes, and Greek, for both translation and private purposes (my wife is Greek). All in all, the training has been quite good, but there have not been enough courses organised in Greek. I have done all the levels and two courses in Greece, but I still have difficulties understanding what the texts are about when reading them normally without looking up words in the dictionary.

What do you enjoy most about being a translator? What do you not enjoy? Would you like to change over to administration? If so, why? If not, why not?
I like working with foreign languages. I enjoy having a concrete task to do every day and always being able to see the results of my work. I also like the fact that normally I have quite regular working hours and that there are no problems circulating in my head when I am off duty, as was the case when I worked as a lawyer. In the long run, it might be a bit unsatisfactory always having to reproduce other people's thoughts and not expressing one's own. As to changing over to administration, it obviously depends on the specific post. I think many people with prejudices about the job as a translator overestimate the interest

of many administrative posts, and I have seen several ex-translators who seemed to have been disappointed with their administrator jobs. In 1998 I worked temporarily as a law clerk (French: *référendaire*) for the Danish president of the Court of First Instance and I was offered the post on a longer term basis, but to many people's surprise I turned the offer down because I did not find it interesting enough to be willing to make the necessary sacrifices concerning my private life. But the mere fact that I was offered the job proved to me that the work of a translator can be appreciated even at the highest level.

Have you worked as a freelance translator?
No.

Can you imagine working as a freelance in future?
I would not exclude it, although I do not think that the institutions should have too high a percentage of translations done by freelance translators. It would all depend on the specific conditions.

Do you have much contact with translation requesters?
Yes, quite a lot, but mostly because I contact them to point out mistakes in the original text.

Do you have enough information about the purpose of translations?
Normally yes.

Do you ever get feedback from end users (e.g. readers in the Member States)?
Hardly ever.

Have you ever complained about the quality of an original text? What was the response?
As I said above, I often contact the authors of the original texts, not to complain, but to help to ensure that the original texts of my institution are as correct as possible. The response is normally very positive and appreciative.

Are there any translation-related activities, apart from actual translation, which you are able to carry out occasionally (terminology work, teaching, lecturing, training colleagues, writing guides for translators, etc.)?
I am involved in tutoring new colleagues and I am a member of several working groups: one created by the Director with colleagues from three other language divisions, dealing with quality control, one on possible changes to our structure, and one that writes guides for translators.

Do you think it would be a good idea to merge all the institutions' translation services into one?

As far as the Court is concerned, I cannot see any point in such a merger, our texts being completely different from those of the other institutions and needing to be translated by lawyers only. In addition, there would be a problem of confidentiality. The judgments of the Court and the opinions of the Advocates General are still confidential when they are being translated, and very often the other institutions are parties in the cases. In general, I find it difficult to see what the advantages of such a merger could be, unless there are unused resources in some of the institutions that could be used in others.

Jyrki Lappi-Seppälä, translator, language coordinator

Profile:

Jyrki Lappi-Seppälä is Finnish; his mother tongue is Finnish and he also knows English, French, Spanish, Swedish, German, Portuguese and some Estonian.

When Finland joined the EU in 1995, he was appointed head of the Finnish translation division in the Joint Services of the Economic and Social Committee and Committee of the Regions. Then in 1997 he moved to the European Commission's translation service, where he is Language Coordinator for Finnish.

In his pre-EU life he was an editor and manager in various publishing houses, a freelance translator, interpreter and language consultant, a language teacher in the Finnish Parliament (teaching Spanish to MPs, among them Tarja Halonen, who was later to become President of Finland), and an aid administrator in Central America. He is a prize-winning translator of fiction.

You started working for the EU institutions when Finland joined the EU in 1995. Was it a culture shock for Finns, coming to Brussels?

If you mean by "Brussels" the multicultural working environment in the EU institutions, I was not particularly surprised, since I had worked in several international bodies and headed a field office for development co-operation. The French-style administrative culture of the EU was of course a new experience, only comparable to my 8-month service in the Finnish Armed Forces during the mid-60s.

But if you mean by Brussels the actual capital of Belgium, the shock was greater. I had never expected to face in the "Capital of Europe" the daily difficulties, deficient public services and inefficiency with which I had become so familiar in "real" under-developed countries, where they were far more understandable.

Now you have worked in two different EU bodies, the Joint Services and the

Commission – one quite small, and one much larger. How do the two of them compare?

I must say that the atmosphere in a small institution was cosy and pleasant compared with a huge faceless machine like the Commission. But for me, as a linguist who wants to influence and improve the use of my mother tongue in EU documents, in close interaction with different institutions in Finland and with colleagues in other EU bodies, the Commission seems to be the right place to work.

Your present post at the Commission is "Language Coordinator for Finnish". What does a language coordinator do?

The language coordinator has multiple tasks. My tasks include: dealing with open competitions for the recruitment of Finnish translators, participating in the recruitment of new colleagues, an advisory role in personnel administration matters like promotions and transfers, regular contacts with Finnish universities, research centres and authorities in language questions, organising training placements here for Finnish translation students and graduates, giving lectures to visitors and the Finnish public, organising training in Finnish for Finnish translators and giving general linguistic guidance in Finnish.

Why did you become a translator?

Languages have always been my passion. I studied four languages at school and started to learn Spanish when I was a student, first in evening classes in Helsinki and then on summer courses in Spain. I was 18 when I started my first book translation from Brazilian Portuguese (Jorge Amado). Part of my passion for languages may have been in my genes, or at least it may go back to childhood experiences and surroundings, since my mother was a teacher, my grandfather was a lecturer in Latin and Greek, a poet and etymologist, and my grandmother was also a translator.

Was it a deliberate career choice?

It was, indeed! I always knew I wanted to be a translator. Although I have had several jobs in private business (mainly publishing), all of them have had to do in some way or other with languages, culture and cross-cultural communication.

Did you have specific university training as a translator?

During my university studies in the 60s and 70s, translation was not yet an academic discipline. I majored in general linguistics, which was dominated at the time by Noam Chomsky and his "generative grammar", but translation theories were also widely discussed. So at university I didn't actually learn how to translate, but I did learn what translation is about.

*Since starting work here, have you learnt any new languages? Which ones?
Was it for professional or social reasons? Were you happy with the language
training provided?*
I recently started a Commission course in Estonian, a language I had already
made some acquaintance with back in the remote 60s. This was mainly for professional reasons, because I can imagine having a role in helping the Estonian
translators adjust to work here; maybe I could share with them my experience
of the Finnish accession from the language point of view. I am happy with the
course, because it is specifically for linguists.

*Have you worked as a freelance translator? Can you imagine working as a
freelance in future?*
Besides my several permanent jobs I have practised fiction translation uninter-
ruptedly from 1964, and I intend to continue doing so after my retirement.

*Do you have much contact with translation requesters? Do you have enough
information about the purpose of translations?*
As a language coordinator I am not involved in the daily production process,
and contacts with the requesters are handled by other staff, but I know that such
contacts are more and more frequent. The requesters are usually quite helpful,
although there are also examples of the contrary, and sometimes it is hard to
reach the right person. The purpose (target public) of the text is rarely indicated, which makes it difficult to choose the right translation strategy and style
register.
    More than once, changes have been made to a foggy original on the basis of
suggestions made by Finnish translators. Due to its non-Indo-European structure, the Finnish language often serves as an acid test for the translatability of a
text or a new term. Suppose someone wants to launch a term like "social
unadaptability". The speakers of Indo-European languages don't necessarily
need to analyse or even fully understand what is meant by the new term; they
can simply transpose it to their own language using the Greco-Latin "term
generator": FR *inadaptabilité sociale*, ES *inadaptabilidad social*, PT *inadapt-
abilidade social* etc. But the Finns need to know whether "social" refers here to
society as a system or to behavioural aspects, and whether the verb "adapt" is
meant to have an active or reflexive meaning ("to adapt something to something" or "to adapt oneself to something"). So we cannot just absorb unclear
concepts without being able to analyse them.

Do you ever get feedback from end users (e.g. readers in the Member States)?
I often receive feedback from Finland. The public and the authorities in a relatively new member state are quite sensitive to language questions, and during
the first years of Finland's membership of the EU, the quality of Finnish

translations was frequently criticised in the press. At present, the public and the authorities seem to be satisfied with the quality on the whole. Every now and then, of course, we receive negative feedback on individual translations.

Do you think it would be a good idea to merge all the institutions' translation services into one?
With some reservations, yes, provided that the hierarchical structure is flexible enough and that relatively autonomous sections for each institution are maintained. The staff could in principle continue translating for a given institution, but would be ready to give mutual assistance during peak situations. The horizontal and support services could be shared or at least subject to overall coordination. In my job as language coordinator, at any rate, I feel there is an imperative need for more structured interinstitutional cooperation.

Clare Sholl, freelance translator

Profile:
Clare Sholl is British; her mother tongue is English and she also knows Norwegian, Swedish, Danish and German. She is a freelance translator specialising in the areas of food, agriculture and the environment. She has also worked as an in-house translator for Reuters in the UK, spending about 18 months there abstracting financial stories from Austrian, Swiss, Dutch and Scandinavian newspapers.

She coordinates the EU information network of freelance translators in the Institute of Translation and Interpreting (ITI) in the United Kingdom. She lives in Frankfurt, Germany.

Her background in agriculture includes training in the Agriculture DG at the European Commission (working on the 1993/94 enlargement negotiations with Austria, Finland, Norway and Sweden). In addition she has experience in food-related journalism and has diplomas in EU Law and Public International Law, as well as having studied International Environmental Law.

She is currently taking a break from translation to concentrate upon looking after her 2 year old daughter.

What is the purpose of the EU information network that you coordinate for the ITI?
The purpose of the ITI EU network is to provide a pool of information for linguists interested in EU work, whether translation or interpreting, freelance or in-house. It is intended to encourage an exchange of experience and to highlight opportunities for professional development. The ultimate aim is to help

translators improve the quality of their work and aid the flow of information between work providers and freelancers. The increased contact between individuals and companies should also provide more scope for 'match-making' between agencies and sub-contractors or freelancers wishing to form groupings.

Do the freelance translators in the network all translate into English?
No, since not all of the members of the ITI in the UK translate into English.

Do you have any contact with similar networks in other countries?
I am not aware of the existence of similar networks but would be very interested in forming contacts with any that do exist.

What sort of problems do freelance translators have in their work for the EU translation services?
The problems highlighted so far have been invoicing requirements (invoices being returned because they were incorrectly worded) and the confusion over which style guide/dictionary to use when, something which a couple of network members have researched and written about for the network. The network is still very new so hopefully people will come forward with any other problems they may have for discussion and feedback.

Do you think they understand the difference between the different institutions (for example, the difference between the European Commission and the Translation Centre)?
It would appear that network members already working for the institutions have a good understanding of the differences between the different institutions. One aim of the network is to clear up any confusion on this or other matters which may exist among translators wishing to embark upon this type of work.

Why did you become a translator?
Having studied languages (German and Scandinavian) and done some in-house work while still an undergraduate, translation was always an obvious option. However, I ventured down a few other avenues first! I then found that I could combine using languages with my interests in the EU, food, agriculture and the environment by working freelance for the Commission.

Was it a deliberate career choice?
Yes. Translation was the ideal way for me to work with languages, law and agriculture.

Did you have any specific university training as a translator?
I have the Institute of Linguists Diploma in Translation for German into

English, which I sat after attending a course at City University in London.

What do you enjoy most about being a translator? What do you not enjoy?
I enjoy combining a variety of skills and interests and being able to keep pace with developments in several areas of EU policy. The one drawback, particularly with freelance work, is that I would like more face-to-face contact with other people.

Have you worked as an in-house (staff) translator? Would you like to, or do you prefer being freelance? If so, why?
I am fortunate to have experience of both in-house and freelance work. I preferred working freelance because I was doing more interesting work but also it allowed me to work alongside looking after a young child (I found the institutions very flexible in respect of maternity leave etc). It is nice to feel part of an in-house team, though, and I may decide to return to in-house work at some point in the future.

Do you have much contact with the translation requesters? Do you have enough information about the purpose of translations? Do you ever get feedback from end users (e.g. readers in the Member States)?
I have always found that my contacts in the translation service have been able to answer any queries. I know that requesters may prove more elusive as they are often in meetings etc. as well. The nature of the work I have done means that it is usually clear that texts are for internal consumption (e.g. information supplied by the Member States at the request of the Commission). I have never had feedback from end users.

Have you ever complained about the quality of an original text? What was the response?
No, I have not needed to complain as I generally translate from Swedish and Danish and the Scandinavians tend to write well.

What proportion of your work was for the EU institutions? Are other clients more helpful, more generous with fees, or faster payers?
Over the past couple of years all of my work has been for the EU institutions. My past experience of working for agencies has been that they were less helpful (as they were less involved in / knowledgeable about the areas I specialise in). For this reason I found it a lot more rewarding to work directly with the institutions and I have particularly enjoyed working with Graham Riley and Ivor Bloor from the Commission's Translation Service who have offered me much advice and encouragement. Also the high standard demanded by the institutions

has helped further my professional development and given me a lot of pride in my work.

I charged the institutions less than I charged agencies because I preferred to work directly and was determined to be given the opportunity to do EU work. Agencies paid me more quickly (I only allowed a one month payment period), although a couple did not pay at all until I threatened legal action ... I have felt more financial security working for an international organisation.

Do you think it would be a good idea to merge all the institutions' translation services into one?
Yes, there would clearly be advantages to this but it would be essential for the service to maintain its strong links with requesters and to continue to be organised according to the different specialist areas relating to the different institutions and policy areas.

Interviews with some users of the translation services

Michiel van Hulten, Member of the European Parliament

Profile:
Michiel van Hulten is Dutch; his mother tongue is Dutch and he speaks English, French and German. He is a Member of the Socialist Group in the European Parliament and represents the Dutch regions of Flevoland and Overijssel. He has a special interest in the administrative reform of the European Union institutions.

He was responsible for the European Parliament's response to the second report of the Committee of Independent Experts. This Committee was set up in 1999 to investigate allegations of fraud and mismanagement in the European Commission.

Before being elected as an MEP in 1999, at the relatively young age of 30, he was an administrator in the Council of the European Union and private secretary to the Dutch Minister of Education, Culture and Science.

Members of the European Parliament must be permitted to speak their mother tongue in Parliament debates, and read background documents in that language. Do you agree with this statement?
I feel that the ability to understand English and/or French is an essential precondition to being an effective MEP. I therefore do not feel that it is essential that MEPs should be able to speak their own mother tongue in Parliamentary debates, although I realise that this is not a tenable position under present conditions.

Will this approach be sustainable after enlargement, with the addition of up to 12 official languages?
I support the introduction of a system whereby MEPs can speak in their own language, but must listen in a limited number of working languages.

You have made proposals to modify the European Parliament's language arrangements after enlargement. What are they? Are they transferable to other institutions? Or do you have alternative suggestions for the other institutions?
The European Parliament should introduce a system whereby *interpretation* is out of all languages, and only into two or three languages (English, French and German) [This is referred to as the SALT system – Speak All, Listen Three]. *Translation* should involve only two or three working languages; only final texts should be translated into all languages. My view on the Commission is that it should use two working languages only, English and French. The Council should also use only English and French, except at ministerial level.

As a user of the European Parliament's translation service, are you satisfied with the service provided?
Yes – I think it's very good.

Do you think the translations are generally accurate? In style, are they too administrative-sounding? Or too "journalistic"?
I think the translations are, in general, very good. When there are shortcomings, it is because they are too administrative-sounding rather than too journalistic. An additional problem for Dutch documents is that Flemish translators often use different terms than their Dutch colleagues – terms which can sound odd to mother-tongue Dutch readers.

What do you think is more important: delivery on time, or quality?
This partly depends on the stage of the process. In the final stages, after a text has been voted on, quality is probably more important. Before votes are taken, speed is probably slightly more important.

Have you ever experienced problems arising from translations (written translations as opposed to interpretation), such as misunderstandings arising during a meeting, and time wasted as a result; or cancellation of an important meeting because the translations were not available in time?
There have been fewer problems then I would have expected, but that is largely thanks to MEPs and staff being flexible. If the rules were strictly adhered to, there would be severe disruption of Parliament's work, primarily because not all language versions of a text are available in time (or, in the case of compromise amendments for instance, at all).

Have you ever contacted the translation service to discuss these problems or (in the absence of problems) to thank them for the good service provided?
I have never thanked them for the service provided. This is partly due to their anonymity. Your question leads me to suggest that perhaps the names of translators should be mentioned on translated documents. The same goes for interpreters. An interesting difference between Council and Parliament is that in Council, interpreters are literally more visible than in the EP: here, they are hidden behind glass that is very dark. That results in less personal contact.

Have you ever done any translations yourself? Why? Did you enjoy it?
I invariably write my own documents and amendments in English, in order to make sure that the version most used is the one I wrote myself. I have also done some translation work: for instance, I translated the Party of European Socialists 1999 election manifesto from English into Dutch.

Do you ever use machine translation? What do you think of it?
I have not. When I tried to as a Council administrator, the language combination I sought was not yet available.

Do you think the public image of the European Parliament is affected by translation?
I think it can sometimes reinforce the image of a place that is not entirely in touch with its surroundings.

Do you think it would be a good idea to merge all the institutions' translation services into one?
Given the similarity of the work carried out, yes I do. I am also not opposed in principle to outsourcing translation work on the basis of competitive tendering.

Hans Brunmayr, Deputy Director General at the Council of the European Union

Profile:
Hans Brunmayr is Austrian; his mother tongue is German and he knows English, French, Spanish, Dutch, Italian, Portuguese.
  He is the Deputy Director-General for Codecision Procedure, Transparency and Information Policy at the General Secretariat of the Council of the European Union. Before joining the Council shortly after Austria's accession to the European Union in 1995, he worked for almost thirty years in the Austrian Diplomatic Service holding foreign posts at the Austrian Embassies in Paris, Buenos Aires and The Hague. From 1985 he participated in EC-EFTA and EEA negotiations and was a member of the team preparing and conducting the Austrian accession negotiations.

As an Austrian joining the European Union, did you find working practices in Brussels very different from those in Austria?

As a diplomat I was used to working in other countries, in other languages and to adapting to other cultures. In particular, my work in the field of European integration from 1985, with bilateral negotiations between Austria and the Community represented by the Commission, the work within EFTA and later in the EEA and the Austrian accession negotiations gave me a good insight into the working practices in Brussels.

The work in the Council Secretariat coincides in many aspects with my former work as a diplomat and the working practices are quite similar to those in Austria, the main difference being that work in Brussels is carried out in a multinational environment where the views of all 15 Member States have to be taken into account. I consider this multinational culture in the European institutions as one of the major assets of the work in Brussels.

As the person in charge of information policy at the Council, do you feel that the general public has enough access to Council documents? Is enough attention given to the clarity of language?

It goes without saying that further improvements could and should be made to offer easier access to Council documents to the general public. I hope that we will be able in the future to make quite a large percentage of Council documents fully accessible on our Internet website as soon as they are produced. It has to be mentioned that in the field of transparency and access to documents, the Council has made significant progress over the last six years. The statistics show that 87% of all documents requested are now released on demand. The Council was the first institution to create an electronic register of all Council documents in all eleven official languages and since July 2000 also puts the full text of all released documents on the Internet.

The clarity of language used in Council documents and in particular in legal texts certainly leaves considerable room for improvement. We have to pay particular attention to the guidelines on the quality of drafting of Community legislation. This is certainly a very difficult task because compromises can very often only be achieved by using somewhat ambiguous language.

Access to documents is only a small part of transparency and information policy. It is necessary to explain to the public the functioning of the institution and the decisions it takes in easily understandable language.

Is it necessary for each institution to have its own information policy? Wouldn't a single EU information policy be less confusing for outsiders?

Information on the European Union should be considered as a whole, every player contributing in a complementary manner to the overall picture. The present situation is certainly not satisfactory. Too much different and sometimes contradictory information is given. The solution cannot be an independent information policy of the Council, the Commission, the European Parliament and Member States, but a coherent approach with close networking between those responsible for information in institutions and Member States. In this context the role of the General Secretariat of the Council has to be to provide factual information on the Council's activities focusing particularly on the second and third pillars. This information should be made available to information providers in Member States, with the aim being that it is not an anonymous Brussels bureaucracy but someone close to the citizen who gives information about the European-level decisions likely to affect the daily lives of the citizens.

As a user of the Council's translation service, are you satisfied with the service provided?
The answer is a clear 'yes'. It has always been possible to accommodate our needs even under very difficult circumstances at moments when the translation services were flooded with demands from the various DGs and under pressure from the Council presidencies.

Do you think the translations are generally accurate? In style, are they too administrative-sounding? Or too "journalistic"?
I think the translations are generally accurate. As the texts I am dealing with are mostly of a legal character, the danger of too journalistic translations does not exist. Sometimes terminology problems arise but they can always be solved easily by direct contacts.

What do you think is more important: delivery on time, or quality?
Quality is certainly more important. However the big challenge and difficult task for the translation services is very often to produce a top-quality text within a very short time. This is regularly the case before the end of the year, when many legal acts which need to be implemented by 1 January have to be finalised and adopted.

Have you ever experienced problems arising from translations (written translations as opposed to interpretation), such as misunderstandings arising during a meeting, and time wasted as a result; or cancellation of an important meeting because the translations were not available in time?
I have experienced some problems from translations which did not fully coincide in all eleven languages. This happened mainly in codecision procedures with the European Parliament, where texts are sometimes translated by translation services of three different institutions. These misunderstandings could always be easily resolved by taking the language in which the relevant text had been drafted as a reference.

I have never been confronted with cancellation of an important meeting because translations were not available in time. On the other hand I am regularly confronted with the limited capacity of interpretation services, which makes the organisation of Conciliation Committee meetings between the European Parliament and the Council, where two full interpretation teams are needed, extremely difficult.

Have you ever contacted the translation service to discuss these problems or (in the absence of problems) to thank them for the good service provided?
I have regular contacts with the director of the Council's translation services and his deputy in order to discuss ways and means to make best use of the existing translation capacities and ensure that our needs can be satisfied on time. On these occasions I have always expressed my thanks for the good service provided.

My collaborators, in particular those dealing with codecision dossiers, have frequent direct contacts with the translators in charge of a given legislative proposal in order to get draft amendments translated at very short notice or to resolve terminology problems. The translation services have always been very responsive to our demands.

Have you ever done any translations yourself? Why? Did you enjoy it?
In my former work as a diplomat I frequently had to do translations myself from foreign languages into German and vice versa. I always enjoyed this kind of work. In my present function I do translations myself occasionally during negotiations with the European Parliament on new codecision acts.

Do you ever use machine translation? What do you think of it?
I have never used machine translation. I do not think that it is suited to the needs of the Council's work.

Do you think the public image of the Council is affected by translation?
The Council can only take decisions when a text exists in all eleven official languages. Without translations it cannot function. Delays in translations and thus in the taking of a decision by the Council would inevitably have a very negative impact on the public image of the Council. Translations are also fundamental to the Council's work in the field of information. All our publications have to be available in eleven languages. It is sometimes difficult to get all translations for information leaflets at the same time and I am aware that these texts are not necessarily the first priority. However, for the perception of the Council by the public, it is crucial to provide texts in the information field in all languages.

Do you think it would be a good idea to merge all the institutions' translation services into one?
No, a merger would complicate planning and programming of work and would probably affect the quality of translations. Close contacts between the department responsible and the coordinator in the translation service would be hampered. In my view, emphasis should rather be put on development of closer working relations. Specialisation of translators should be facilitated by encouraging temporary secondment of translators to author departments.

David O'Sullivan, Secretary-General of the European Commission

Profile:
David O'Sullivan is Irish; his mother tongue is English and he knows French, German, Spanish, Japanese and Irish.

He is the Secretary-General of the Commission (arguably the most important civil servant in the institution), having formerly been Head of President Prodi's Private Office, and before that, Director-General of the Education and Training DG, Director of Resources in the Employment DG, Deputy Head of Padraig Flynn's Private Office, Head of Unit for the COMETT and TEMPUS training programmes, and a member of Peter Sutherland's cabinet. He also spent four years in the Commission's delegation in Japan.

In 1998 he was in charge of DECODE, a major review of the Commission's services, including the Translation Service.

Did you learn anything new about the Translation Service when you conducted the 1998 review? Did it change your perceptions of translators in any way?
I have always had the highest respect for translators. Their love of language and attention to detail is a very special skill. Given that much of our image passes through language, the role of translation in communicating our work is fundamental. My generally positive impressions were reinforced when I conducted the 1998 DECODE review. What particularly struck me was the dedication of translators to their work, the fact that they sometimes feel frustrated because their work is not adequately recognised, and the fact that they are not sufficiently associated at an earlier stage in the preparation of documents.

Before that, when you worked in the Employment DG and others, did you experience problems with the translation service? Do you think that some problems arise, perhaps, because requesters of translations do not plan ahead and are then surprised that translations can't be delivered as rapidly as they would like?

I have never experienced any problems with the translation service, other than an occasional difficulty linked to the sheer capacity to handle the work in a very tight timeframe; I have always found the service extremely helpful. I fully agree that better planning would be useful. Having a constructive dialogue with the translators at an early stage can smooth the way considerably.

What do you think is the main problem facing translators now (apart from enlargement, which we do not see as a problem)? Might it perhaps be the excessive length of Commission documents? What are you doing, as Secretary General, to try to cut down the length of documents?

I think that the main problem facing translators is the poor quality of many original documents, which are often written by non-native speakers; what is hard to understand in the first place is inevitably more difficult to translate! This means that we need to do more to improve the quality of our original texts. I believe that the translation service itself can play a role here, for example by providing an editing service before documents are translated. We obviously also need to do more to control the length of documents, and to be more discriminating about which documents we translate into 11 languages. This is clearly a sensitive area, but something that we should continue to discuss with the Council.

As a user of the Commission's translation service, are you satisfied with the service provided?

Yes. I have always found the translation service very dedicated and hardworking.

Do you think the translations are generally accurate? In style, are they too administrative-sounding? Or too "journalistic"?

I very rarely read documents in languages other than the original French or English, so I cannot really judge, but the quality of the translation in these languages is certainly good.

What do you think is more important: delivery on time, or quality?

This is a trick question! During my interviews with the translation service someone reminded me of the American saying that you can have any two of the following three things: quick, cheap and good! While I can understand the frustration caused by having to do quick translations which are necessarily of lower quality, I also understand that the services need speed and that we all face resource limitations – so choices have to be made. Of course, if the initial quality of the text is higher, it is easier to reconcile the three!

Have you ever experienced problems arising from translations (written

translations as opposed to interpretation), such as misunderstandings arising during a meeting, and time wasted as a result; or cancellation of an important meeting because the translations were not available in time?
Yes, I have had to postpone meetings because translations were not available, and I have, occasionally, seen political problems arise due to errors in translations.

Have you ever contacted the translation service to discuss these problems or (in the absence of problems) to thank them for the good service provided?
When I have been particularly satisfied with the service provided by the translation service I have tried to send a note of thanks – perhaps not as often as I should have!

Have you ever done any translations yourself? Why? Did you enjoy it?
Yes, in my early days as a civil servant I often used to help colleagues with English translations of texts. I enjoyed it, but not to the point of wanting to become a full-time translator! I do not think that I have the patience or the eye for detail that it requires.

Do you ever use machine translation? What do you think of it?
Yes, I have used Systran, which is a helpful tool to give you a quick overview of a document, even though the machine language that it produces can sometimes give odd results.

Do you think the public image of the Commission is affected by translation?
Of course. Just as good translations ensure that people understand what the Commission is trying to do, poor-quality translations can lead to misunderstandings.

Do you think it would be a good idea to merge all the institutions' translation services into one?
I believe that there is a good deal of scope for interinstitutional cooperation in matters such as translation, and it is certainly hard to explain to the outside world why each institution needs to have a separate translation service. That said, I can also understand the need for some specific in-house capacity for each institution, and the economies of scale of merging translation services would have to be balanced against the risks of creating an excessively large administrative structure that would be hard to manage. Generally speaking, I do not think that we have sufficiently explored the possibilities for cooperation, such as shifting workload across the institutions at peak moments, although I understand that cooperation with the European Parliament has intensified recently.

Works cited

Heidegger, Martin (1954) *Einführung in die Metaphysik*. Tübingen: Niemeyer.

Kennedy, Tom (1998) *Learning European Law: A Primer and Vade-medum*. London: Sweet & Maxwell.

Ortega y Gasset, José (1970) 'The Misery and Splendour of Translation', in *Obras Completas,* Volume 5 (1933-1941). Madrid: Revista de Occidente. 433-452.

Robinson, Douglas (1997) *Western Translation Theory from Herodotus to Nietzsche*. Manchester: St Jerome.

Index